وَمَا أَرْسَلْنَاكَ إِلَّا رَحْمَةً لِّلْعَالَمِينَ

Mercy to Mankind

صَلَّى اللهُ عَلَيْهِ وَسَلَّم

Dr. Abidullah Ghazi
Dr. Tasneema Ghazi

IQRA' International Educational Foundation

Part of a Comprehensive and Systematic Program of Islamic Studies

A Textbook for the program of Sirah

Mercy To Mankind:
Makkah Period

Chief Program Editors
Dr. Abidullah Ghazi
(Ph.D., Study of Religion
Harvard University)
Dr. Tasneema Ghazi
(Ph.D., Curriculum-Reading
University of Minnesota)

Editing
Huseyin Abiva
Dilshad Ali
Aisha Qidwae

Maps
Huseyin Abiva

Design and Layout
Aliuddin Khaja

Revised Expanded Edition, January 2012
Printed in India

IQRA' International Educational Foundation
7450 Skokie Blvd., Skokie, IL 60077
Tel: 847-673-4072 Fax: 847-673-4095
Website: www.iqra.org

LCCN:
ISBN # 1-56316-154-0

IQRA's Note

It is with great happiness that we present this new, completely revised and expanded edition of IQRA's popular textbook, Mercy to Mankind Part I. This textbook was first published in 1980 and has since ran into numerous reprintings.

We are thankful to Allah ﷻ for His guidance and our Ansar and supporters for their assistance in the completion of this valuable work. This book is nothing less than the product of the love and devotion that we hold for our beloved Prophet Muhammad ﷺ. It is our deepest desire that all of our readers, no matter what their age, will enjoy the blessings of reading this *Sirah*, the life story of the Prophet ﷺ.

These days it is important that we refresh ourselves with the significance of the *Sirah* and strive to implement it as a model in our own lives.

This revised and expanded edition of Mercy to Mankind I includes the following distinctive features:

1. Twelve new lessons dealing with the noble personality of Rasulullah ﷺ and some of his *Ahadith* are added.
2. A focal point now introduces each lesson under the heading "Looking Ahead."
3. Students are challenged to use critical thinking skills during their study of the text.
4. Qur'anic teachings are integrated into each lesson.
5. Geography skills are incorporated into the text by means of attractive and topographically accurate maps of the many places of historical importance in the *Sirah*.
6. The book has been attractively designed and printed in color.

We pray that this work, Mercy to Mankind I, will instill feelings of love and devotion for the Noble Prophet ﷺ into the hearts and minds of our readers, encouraging them to follow his *Sunnah* with both right thoughts and right actions.

Dr. Abidullah Ghazi
Executive Director
IQRA' International Educational Foundation
July 15, 2009

About this book
The highlights of this textbook include the following:

Looking Ahead
This boxed feature gets the student ready to take on each lesson by providing a brief synopsis of its content.

Illustrations and Maps
Full color illustrations with detailed and geographically accurate maps will encourage students to take deeper appreciation of the topic being discussed..

Side Bars and Critical Thinking Skills
These features enhance the core material of the text by providing the student with multi-layered contextualization and wider perspectives on the subject matter

Words to Know
This feature introduces the new words and Islamic vocabulary used in the lesson.

Qur'an/Hadith
Connection: Each lesson concludes with either a single *Ayah* or *Hadith* intended to encapsulate the relevance of the lesson's message beyond the historical event.

Sample page (Lesson 2)

Lesson 2

A brief outline of the life of Rasulullah ﷺ

Looking Ahead
Rasulullah ﷺ lived for 63 years. His life was a model for us on how to live a good life and gain Allah's blessings.

Rasulullah s is Allah's last messenger and prophet. Allah ﷻ sent His last book to us - the Qur'an - through the Prophet Muhammad ﷺ. He is the best of all human beings, an ideal man, and a model of how we should be as well. He was perfect in everything he did.

Rasulullah put into practice what he taught. He demonstrated how to live out what is taught in the Qur'an. His way is called the *Sunnah*, or "Prophetic Tradition." It is the duty of every Muslim to try to follow the Prophet's *Sunnah* to the best of his or her ability.

Rasulullah s explained the teachings of the Qur'an to us as well. The reports of his teachings, as well as his sayings are called *Hadiths*. In the centuries after the passing of Rasulullah ﷺ a number of outstanding scholars began to collect these reports. The *Hadiths* were then collected

Sunnah means a "walked path." The *Sunnah* of the Prophet s can mean "the way" of the Prophet. The *Sunnah* is the way or deeds of the Prophet s as narrated, recorded and followed by his Companions. It is our duty to follow the *Sunnah* as we live out our lives. Following the *Sunnah* in everything we say and do will keep us on the straight path and bring Allah's blessings to us.

5

Sample page (We Have Learned)

WE HAVE LEARNED:

- Abrahan, the king of Yemen wanted to destroy the Ka'bah
- Allah ﷻ protected the Ka'bah and destroyed the army
- Muhammad's father died several months before his birth
- Muhammad ﷺ was born on Monday, the 12th of month
- The name "Muhammad" means "Praised One."

WORDS TO KNOW:

Expecting, Fir'awn, Heartbroken, Praise, *Rabi' al-Awwal*

Sample page (Qur'an Connection)

QUR'AN CONNECTION:
Let us read about what Allah says about the Year of the Elephant in the Qur'an:

"Have you not seen how your Lord dealt with the companions of the elephant? Did He not bring their plan to nothing? And He sent against them flocks of birds, striking them with stones of baked clay. Then did He make them like a field of stalks and straw which has been eaten up."
(Sura al-Fil 105:1)

18

Sample page (right)

and asked him, "O my friend! Tell me what you have seen and heard." Rasulullah ﷺ told him what had happened in the cave. Then Waraqa said, "By the Lord in whose hands is my life! You are certainly the nabi, the prophet! Without doubt you have seen the same angel who came to Musa. But the people of Makkah will become your enemies, and they will trouble you. I am very old now and I am sure I won't live much longer. But if I were younger, I would have helped you." Then Waraqa kissed of Rasulullah's forehead and the two men parted company.

There were two major religions in the Middle East at the time of the coming of Islam. These were Christianity and Zoroastrianism.

The beginning of revelation took place in the month of Ramadan as Allah ﷻ has told us in Surah Baqarah, Ayah 185:

"The month of Ramadan is that in which the Qur'an was revealed, guidance to humanity and clear proof of the counseling and the criterion..."
(al-Baqara 2:185)

Waraqa was amazed when he heard this news. He knew that the holy books of the Christians and the Jews predicted the coming of a great prophet and the end of times. He said, "O Khadijah! If you are telling me the truth, then the great angel who visited Musa has now come to your husband. It could be that he is that great prophet whom Allah promised to send."

Then Waraqa continued, "But you must tell him to be steadfast in his belief."

Later Waraqa met Rasulullah ﷺ at the Ka'bah while he was doing his Tawwaf

47

The publication of this book was made possible through a donation from the family of Qazi Alauddin Ahmed Saheb with the intention of Isal Ath-Thawab (إيصال الثواب) for him.

Please remember him and all the believers in your *Du'a'*.

Table of Contents

Table of Contents

A Mercy sent to Mankind

Looking Ahead

Rasulullah ﷺ was sent to us as a mercy from Allah ﷻ. He is the guide to peace and happiness. Let's read in this lesson more about Rasulullah ﷺ!

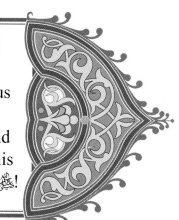

This is the story of the messenger of God, Muhammad ﷺ, the son of 'Abdullah. He was no ordinary man. Allah ﷻ had given him a special mission. The Qur'an instructs Prophet Muhammad ﷺ of his unique task:

وَمَآ أَرْسَلْنَاكَ إِلَّا رَحْمَةً لِّلْعَالَمِينَ ۝

"We have sent you as a mercy to all."
(Surah al-Anbiya' 21:107)

Therefore, the blessed Prophet Muhammad ﷺ is not a prophet only for a selected group of individuals. He is a prophet for the people of all nations, races and cultures. He is the prophet for all people.

In gratefulness to our Prophet ﷺ, we must always ask for the blessings of Allah ﷻ to be upon him. For that reason whenever we hear his name we say:

صلّى الله عليه وسلّم

Sall Allahu 'alaihi wa Sallam
or
May the peace and Blessings of Allah be upon him!

Since we are Muslims it is important that we show our greatest love and respect for Prophet Muhammad ﷺ. When we hear his blessed name we must say,
"Sall Allahu 'alaihi wa Sallam."

This Arabic phrase means, "May the peace and blessings of Allah be upon him." When we ask Allah ﷻ to bless Rasulullah ﷺ, then Allah, the angels, and Rasulullah ﷺ send blessings back to us.

In this book, Mercy to Mankind, we have written " ﷺ " whenever the name of Rasulullah ﷺ is mentioned. This "ﷺ" is a reminder for us to say,
   "Salla Allahu 'alaihi wa Sallam."
We can say this phrase out loud or silently, for Allah ﷻ certainly hears us whether we speak out loud or to ourselves. Either way it is important that we increase our love for Rasulullah ﷺ.

Allah ﷻ sent many prophets and messengers to humankind throughout history. As Muslims we believe in all the prophets as well as the messages they brought. All prophets were special individuals who taught one single religion: Islam, which is submission to the One God. They taught us to worship and submit to One God alone. They taught their people to do good deeds and encourage others to do good deeds. They warned their people against doing wrong both to themselves and to others.

However, as time passed most people did not take notice of the teachings of their

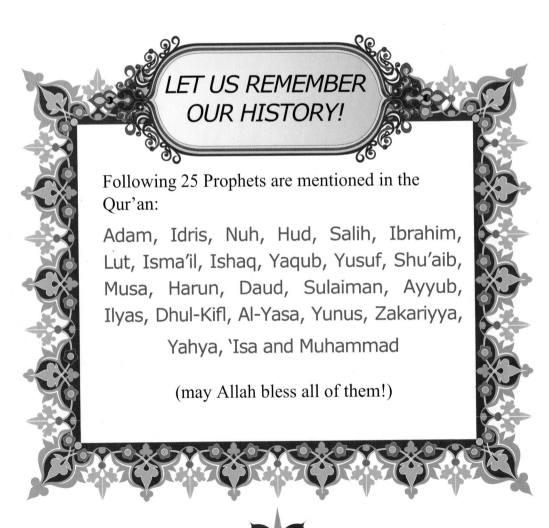

LET US REMEMBER OUR HISTORY!

Following 25 Prophets are mentioned in the Qur'an:

Adam, Idris, Nuh, Hud, Salih, Ibrahim, Lut, Isma'il, Ishaq, Yaqub, Yusuf, Shu'aib, Musa, Harun, Daud, Sulaiman, Ayyub, Ilyas, Dhul-Kifl, Al-Yasa, Yunus, Zakariyya, Yahya, 'Isa and Muhammad

(may Allah bless all of them!)

prophets. Some careless individuals even started to change the books and laws that Allah ﷻ had revealed to His prophets. They did this for their own reasons.

Many also began to turn their attention from Allah ﷻ and they started believing in many gods and goddesses. Worshipping anything other than Allah ﷻ is called *shirk*. The act of *shirk* is not liked by Allah ﷻ because it denies Him His right as our Creator and Master. Our beloved Rasulullah ﷺ came to take away *shirk* from the minds of people. He also came to bring the final message of Allah ﷻ to humankind.

By way of his life, Rasulullah ﷺ let us see how to worship our Creator. He showed us how to show respect to all of creation. It is a mercy from Allah ﷻ that we believe in Prophet Muhammad ﷺ and that we have him to teach us how to be virtuous. Rasulullah ﷺ loved all humanity and successfully completed his mission of conveying Allah's final message to humankind.

Many prophets came before Prophet Muhammad ﷺ, yet he is the very last prophet sent from Allah ﷻ. All the prophets of the past were sent to warn and guide a specific nation or people, but Prophet Muhammad ﷺ was sent to all humanity:

"And We have not sent you except as a bearer of good news and warner unto all mankind. But most of mankind knows not."
(Surah Saba' 34:28)

As Muslims, we belong to the *Ummah* of Rasulullah ﷺ. This means that it is our duty to share the message of Islam with others. Wherever we live we must show people the beauty of Islam through our good behavior. Like Rasulullah ﷺ we must respect all people regardless of their race or religion. We must treat everyone with kindness. We must cooperate with all people to do good deeds, but we must keep away from being in the company of those who follow *Shaitan*.

وَمَآ أَرْسَلْنَٰكَ إِلَّا كَآفَّةً لِّلنَّاسِ بَشِيرًا وَنَذِيرًا وَلَٰكِنَّ أَكْثَرَ ٱلنَّاسِ لَا يَعْلَمُونَ ﴿٢٨﴾

WE HAVE LEARNED:

- When we ask Allah ﷻ to bless Rasulullah ﷺ, great blessings come to us.
- Allah ﷻ does not like the act of *shirk*.
- We must respect all of Allah's creations.

WORDS TO KNOW:

Shirk, Commit, Submit, Virtuous, Worship.

القرآن

QUR'AN CONNECTION:

In the Qur'an Allah ﷻ tells us about the great love that Rasulullah ﷺ has for humanity:

لَقَدْ جَآءَكُمْ رَسُولٌ مِّنْ أَنفُسِكُمْ عَزِيزٌ عَلَيْهِ مَا عَنِتُّمْ حَرِيصٌ عَلَيْكُم بِٱلْمُؤْمِنِينَ رَءُوفٌ رَّحِيمٌ ﴿١٢٨﴾

"There has come to you a messenger from among yourselves, grievous to him is your suffering and he is concerned for you; For the believers he is full of compassion and mercy."

(Surah at-Tawbah 9:128)

A Brief Outline of the Life of Rasulullah ﷺ

Lesson 2

Looking Ahead

Rasulullah ﷺ lived for 63 years. His life was a model for us on how to live a good life and gain Allah's blessings.

Rasulullah ﷺ is Allah's last messenger and prophet. Allah ﷻ sent His last book to us - the Qur'an - through Prophet Muhammad ﷺ. He is the best of all human beings, an ideal man and a model of how we should be as well. He was perfect in everything he did.

Rasulullah ﷺ put into practice what he taught. He demonstrated how to live out what is taught in the Qur'an. His way of life is called the *Sunnah* or "Prophetic Tradition." It is the duty of every Muslim to try to follow the Prophet's *Sunnah* to the best of his or her ability.

Rasulullah ﷺ explained the teachings of the Qur'an to us as well. The reports of his teachings, as well as his sayings are called *Ahadith*. In the centuries after the passing of Rasulullah ﷺ a number

Sunnah means a "walked path." The *Sunnah* of the Prophet ﷺ can mean "the way" of the Prophet. The *Sunnah* is the way or deeds of the Prophet ﷺ as narrated, recorded and followed by his Companions. It is our duty to follow the *Sunnah* as we live out our lives. Following the *Sunnah* in everything we say and do will keep us on the straight path and bring Allah's blessings to us.

of outstanding scholars began to collect these reports. The *Hadiths* were then collected into many books. All Muslims should study the Qur'an and *Ahadith* completely and try to act upon what they tell us.

Prophet Muhammad ﷺ lived in this world for 63 years. When he was 40 years-old, Allah ﷻ honored him with being a messenger and prophet. Rasulullah ﷺ then began to preach the message of the Qur'an in Makkah. He did this for thirteen years. In the beginning only a few *Makkans* accepted Islam as most *Makkans* opposed Rasulullah. These people mocked him, insulted him and persecuted him.

Eventually, they even planned to kill him. Those who followed Rasulullah ﷺ were ridiculed, tortured and even murdered. May Allah ﷻ reward them all!

Twelve years after our master Muhammad ﷺ was honored with his mission, the people of a town known as Yathrib (later called Madinah) began to embrace Islam. When they saw the troubles that grieved the Muslim community of Makkah, they invited Rasulullah ﷺ and the believers to come and live in Yathrib. Allah ﷻ was pleased with the faith of the people of Yathrib. He asked Rasulullah ﷺ and the

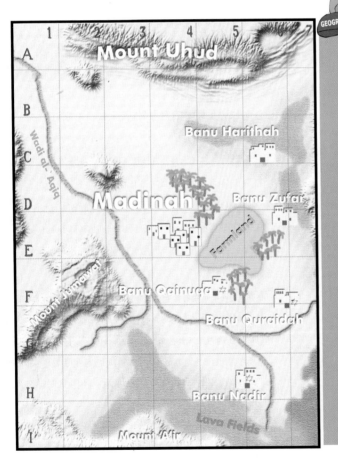

GEOGRAPHY CONNECTION

Look at the map and answer the following questions on a separate piece of paper:

1. Name the tribe which was living closest to the mountain of Uhud.
2. Do you remember the landscape of Makkah? What is the main difference between the geography of Makkah and the geography of Madinah?
3. What kind of fields are found south of the Banu Nadir tribe?
4. Research and write a short report on how lava fields are formed?
5. What tribe is living in grid F5? What was interesting about this tribe?

Muslims to migrate to Madinah, which they did. The Prophet ﷺ established an Islamic state in Madinah with the help of the Muslims.

The *Makkans* attacked the Muslims of Madinah several times with powerful armies. In the beginning the Muslims were few in number. But each time the *Makkans* and their allies attacked, the believers fought bravely. After nearly ten years of struggle, the Muslims were able to march to Makkah and take the city. Rasulullah ﷺ forgave all of those who were his enemies. In this way Allah ﷻ fulfilled His promises to His Messenger and to the believers, and nearly all of Arabia accepted Islam before Rasulullah ﷺ passed away.

Rasulullah ﷺ always worked towards spreading Islam. He suffered much for his mission. He spent his time teaching the Oneness of God, and helping people with their problems. He spent part of every night in prayer by himself. Today we are Muslims only as a result of his efforts. Without Rasulullah ﷺ we would not know what is right and what is wrong.

On the Day of Judgment, Prophet Muhammad ﷺ will ask that Allah's forgiveness be given to all of his *Ummah*. A man once came to Rasulullah ﷺ and asked, "O Messenger of Allah! When is the Last Day coming?" Rasulullah ﷺ answered, "Well, what have you prepared for it?" The man replied, "Not much. I haven't made a lot of prayers or fasted much or given a great deal charity. But

I love Allah and His Messenger." The Prophet ﷺ responded,

"Don't worry then. You will be with the one you love."
(al-Bukhari)

As believers we should love Prophet Muhammad ﷺ more than ourselves, more than our parents, more than our friends, and in fact, more than anyone else. One day 'Umar ibn al-Khattab ﷺ told the Prophet ﷺ, "O Messenger of Allah! I love you more than anyone except my own self." Rasulullah ﷺ answered, "None of you will truly believe until I am dearer than your own self." 'Umar then said, "By the One who sent down the Book to you, I love you more than myself." The Prophet said,

"Ah! Now you have belief 'Umar!"
(al-Bukhari)

Let us all say,

صلّى الله عليه وسلّم

"Salla Allahu 'alaihi wa sallam," and read about the life of Rasulullah ﷺ in this book. He is the most excellent of people, the model human being, the Crown of Allah's creation and the Mercy to Mankind.

WE HAVE LEARNED:

- ☾ Rasulullah ﷺ is the best model for all humankind.
- ☾ We should follow his *Sunnah*.
- ☾ Rasulullah ﷺ spent all his life struggling in the cause of Allah.

WORDS TO KNOW:

Allies, Mock, *Hadith, Sunnah, Ummah,* Ridicule

القرآن

QUR'AN CONNECTION:

In the Qur'an, Allah ﷻ orders Rasulullah ﷺ to say to the believers:

قُلْ إِن كُنتُمْ تُحِبُّونَ ٱللَّهَ فَٱتَّبِعُونِى

يُحْبِبْكُمُ ٱللَّهُ وَيَغْفِرْ لَكُمْ ذُنُوبَكُمْ ۗ وَٱللَّهُ غَفُورٌ رَّحِيمٌ

Say: "If ye do love Allah, Follow me: Allah will love you and forgive you your sins: For Allah is Oft-Forgiving, Most Merciful."
(Surah Al Imran: 31)

Life in Arabia before Islam

Looking Ahead

What was life like in Arabia before Rasulullah ﷺ? Let's learn about the Ka'bah and earlier prophets in this lesson!

Nearly four thousand years ago, Allah ﷻ commanded Prophet Ibrahim ﷺ and his oldest son, Isma'il ﷺ, to make a building dedicated to worshipping One God. This building came to be known as the Ka'bah. It was constructed in an empty desert valley called Makkah. Since the

time of Prophet Ibrahim ﷺ people have been worshipping at the Ka'bah. Allah ﷻ revealed His guidance to Prophet Ibrahim ﷺ and his son Prophet Isma'il ﷺ. These two prophets taught the Arab tribes about *Tawhid*, the oneness of God. They also taught them to do good deeds and stay away from wrong.

However, after Prophet Ibrahim ﷺ and his son Prophet Isma'il ﷺ had passed away, their people forgot most of these teachings. Instead of worshipping Allah ﷻ, they began to worship other things, such as the sun, the moon and the wind. They turned these aspects of nature into gods and goddesses. They made images of these gods out of stone and wood. They filled the Ka'bah with such images and prayed to them. The Ka'bah remained a holy place for the Arabs, but

Prophet Ibrahim ﷺ and his son Isma'il ﷺ built the Ka'bah in the desert valley of Makkah.

they had changed its original purpose. Now they came from all over Arabia to worship the images of their gods and goddesses instead of the One God, Allah ﷻ.

The Gods & Goddesses Of Pre-Islamic Arabia

The Arabs used to worship many different gods and goddesses (some accounts say up to 365). Each deity was believed to have power over a certain aspect of life. Some of the more important ones were:

Hubal Yaghuth
al-Lat Qawm
al-'Uzza Shams
al-Manat
Wadd

The tribes also forgot about the command to do good deeds. They began quarreling among themselves and killing each other. In order to make more money people cheated each other in their business deals. They started drinking alcoholic drinks, which only added to their bad behavior. For entertainment they gambled in games of chance. They abused their slaves and those who had no strong families to protect them. They even stole money from orphans and the poor.

Women in Arabia had few rights and little respect. They were seen as being less valuable than men. Sometimes fathers were so ashamed of having daughters that they would bury their newborn baby girls alive in the desert. Allah ﷻ criticized this very clearly in the Qur'an:

وَإِذَا بُشِّرَ أَحَدُهُم بِٱلْأُنثَىٰ ظَلَّ وَجْهُهُۥ مُسْوَدًّا وَهُوَ كَظِيمٌ ۝ يَتَوَارَىٰ مِنَ ٱلْقَوْمِ مِن سُوءِ مَا بُشِّرَ بِهِۦٓ أَيُمْسِكُهُۥ عَلَىٰ هُونٍ أَمْ يَدُسُّهُۥ فِى ٱلتُّرَابِ أَلَا سَآءَ مَا يَحْكُمُونَ ۝

"And when a daughter is announced to one of them his face becomes black and he is full of wrath. He hides himself from the people because of the evil of that which is announced to him. Shall he keep it with disgrace or bury it (alive) in the dust? Now surely evil is what they judge."

(Surah an-Nahl 16:58-59)

All of the lands that surrounded Arabia were ruled by strong leaders. Unlike the other nations of the earth, the Arab people did not have one powerful king. Instead, they were divided into many tribes.

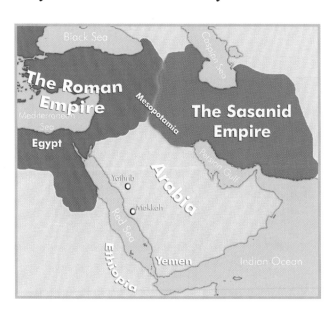

During the Prophet's lifetime, the Middle East was dominated by two powerful empires.

Most of the time these tribes fought each other, sometimes over the smallest things. They stopped fighting only during four special months when many of them went to Makkah for a pilgrimage to the Ka'bah.

These tribes were organized into a hierarchy with the most respected tribes at the top. A hierarchy is an arrangement of people or things into ranks or classes. The most respected tribe in all of Arabia was the Quraish. They were famous as businessmen and as a result, they grew very wealthy. More importantly, they were in charge of the sacred city of Makkah and had the honor of taking care of the Ka'bah.

Eventually, Allah ﷻ sent Prophet Muhammad ﷺ to teach the message of Islam once more to the Arab tribes and the people living beyond Arabia. He was born in the powerful tribe of the Quraish.

Allah ﷻ completed His religion through Muhammad. Rasulullah ﷺ taught the ancient belief in *Tawhid*, that there is no god except One God. He encouraged people to do good not only for themselves but to each other. He encouraged people to avoid wrong actions. He wanted people to do all they could for justice and peace, and to work against unfairness and injustice.

Unlike the prophets before him, Rasulullah ﷺ was sent not only to the Arabs but to all of mankind. Allah ﷻ created humans to be of many colors, nations and tribes, but all of us make up one big family. We must live in peace and kindness with all people. We always have to remember there will be a Day of Judgment when everyone will be brought to life once more. We will then have to answer for all of what we believed and did in this life.

THINK ABOUT IT!

Why do you think the tribe of Quraish was the most respected tribe in Arabia?

Give at least two reasons.

A.

B.

WE HAVE LEARNED:

- The Ka'bah was built by Prophet Ibrahim and Prophet Isma'il ﷺ for the worship of one God alone.
- The people of Arabia forgot the teachings of their prophets and filled the Ka'bah with idols.
- Allah raised Muhammad ﷺ as His last messenger to teach the religion of Islam once again.

WORDS TO KNOW:

Construct, Gamble, Guidance, Hierarchy, Pilgrimage, Tribe

القرآن

QUR'AN CONNECTION:

In the Qur'an Allah ﷻ tells the Muslims that they are to believe in all the prophets and messengers that came before:

قُولُوٓاْ ءَامَنَّا بِٱللَّهِ وَمَآ أُنزِلَ إِلَيۡنَا

وَمَآ أُنزِلَ إِلَىٰٓ إِبۡرَٰهِـۧمَ وَإِسۡمَٰعِيلَ وَإِسۡحَٰقَ وَيَعۡقُوبَ وَٱلۡأَسۡبَاطِ

وَمَآ أُوتِيَ مُوسَىٰ وَعِيسَىٰ وَمَآ أُوتِيَ ٱلنَّبِيُّونَ مِن رَّبِّهِمۡ لَا نُفَرِّقُ

بَيۡنَ أَحَدٍ مِّنۡهُمۡ وَنَحۡنُ لَهُۥ مُسۡلِمُونَ ١٣٦

"Say: We believe in Allah and what was revealed to Muhammad and in what was revealed to Ibrahim, Isma'il, Ishaq, Ya'qub, the tribes of Israel, and that which was given to Musa and 'Isa and what was given to the prophets from their Lord. We make no differences between one and another of them and we submit to Allah alone."

(Surah al-Baqarah 2:136)

A Prophet is Born

Lesson 4

Looking Ahead

The birth of Rasulullah ﷺ is an important event in the history of mankind. Let's read about the events that surrounded his birth.

In the year 570 after the birth of Prophet 'Isa ﷺ, a young man named Abdullah, the son of Abdul Muttalib and Fatima bint Umri, lived in Makkah. He was of the clan of Bani Hashim, which was part of the powerful tribe of Quraish. Abdullah was newly married to a lady named Aminah, who was from a noble family. It was not long after that Aminah was expecting a baby.

Many months before Prophet Muhammad ﷺ was born, the king of Yemen, named Abraha, planned to destroy the Ka'bah. He had built a huge church in his capitol city. He wanted the church to become the center of pilgrimage, not the Ka'bah. He grew angry when he saw that the Arabs ignored the building that he spent so much money on. So Abraha gathered an army and marched over five hundred miles up the Red Sea coast to attack Makkah.

After many weeks of marching through the hot desert, Abraha's army reached Makkah. The Makkans saw hundreds of men armed with spears, swords and bows. They also saw that the Abraha's army had a huge war-elephant called *Fil* in Arabic. The people of the city were frightened, because they did not have an army. Most of them had never even seen an elephant and they may have thought it was some kind of monster.

Being one of the most important citizens of Makkah, Abdul Muttalib decided that it was his responsibility to go out and meet Abraha. Abraha's men had also taken 200 camels that belonged to Abdul Muttalib, and he wanted them back.

13

Miles 0 100 200 300 400

Yathrib

Makkah

The Red Sea

Abraha's March

YEMEN

1. How many miles do you think Abraha's army had to travel from Yemen to reach Makkah?

He went to the tent of the king and said, "Your majesty, I want back my camels your men took." King Abraha was surprised by this request. He thought Abdul Muttalib had come to beg him not to tear down the Ka'bah.

"You are very worried about your camels," he said, "Aren't you concerned about the Ka'bah?" Abdul Muttalib replied, "I am the owner of camels, but the Ka'bah has a protector and He will protect it."

Abraha was upset by this response. "Hah! He won't be able to protect it from me!"

"Well that's between you and Him," answered Abdul Muttalib.

After that Abraha ordered the camels to be returned to Abdul Muttalib. The old Arab chief returned to Makkah and advised everyone to go up into the mountains that surrounded Makkah. There was no way they could defeat Abraha's army. Everyone in the city gathered their families and what little belongings they could and went up into the mountains.

The next morning Abraha ordered his men to attack. They tried to get their elephant to lead the way, but the animal would not move. No matter how hard they beat the elephant, it would not go forward. And then, they all looked up and saw the sky was filled with strange little birds.

The army was frightened when they saw

the sight of thousands of birds flying overhead. Then, the birds began to drop small pebbles from their beaks and claws. Those in the army who were hit died instantly. The men began to run every-where and Abraha's army was destroyed by small birds. The king ordered his men to retreat back to Yemen. Abraha was also struck by the pebbles and died on the way back home.

In this way, the Protector of the Ka'bah definitely defended His house!

After Abraha's army was destroyed the people of Makkah returned to their homes. They carried on with their daily lives having seen a great miracle. From that time on, the Arabs called this year the "Year of the Elephant."

Soon after this great miracle, Abdullah went on a business trip to Yathrib. However, he did not know that he would never see his beloved Makkah again. He became ill and died suddenly on the outskirts of the city. Aminah was heartbroken when she received the news that her husband had died. She was especially worried about the baby she was expecting. "What will become of my child?" she often thought, "My baby will grow up without the loving care of a father."

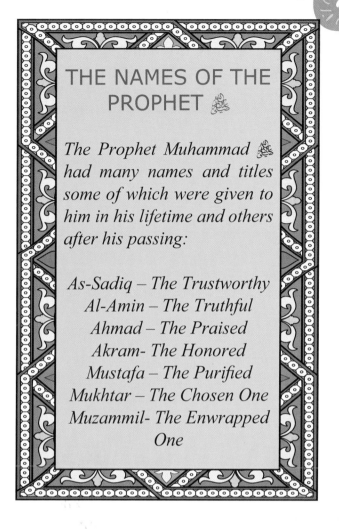

THE NAMES OF THE PROPHET ﷺ

The Prophet Muhammad ﷺ *had many names and titles some of which were given to him in his lifetime and others after his passing:*

As-Sadiq – The Trustworthy
Al-Amin – The Truthful
Ahmad – The Praised
Akram- The Honored
Mustafa – The Purified
Mukhtar – The Chosen One
Muzammil- The Enwrapped One

One night after Abdullah's death, Aminah had a dream. In the dream she saw an angel who told her, "Aminah! Don't worry for your child will be a great man. You will name him Muhammad!" Aminah was full of joy when she woke up. Later on she had more beautiful dreams about her baby. They gave her peace and comfort. She waited eagerly for her baby to be born.

Then on Monday morning, the 12th day of *Rabi' al-Awwal,* 53 years before the *Hijrah*, Aminah gave birth to a baby boy. As the baby was coming into the world, she saw many strange beings. She saw her room filled with the light of angels.

She saw the blessed Lady Maryam ﷺ - the mother of Isa ﷺ - and Lady Asiya, the righteous wife of the Pharaoh. They all came to welcome the baby and wish the new mother well.

Abdul Muttalib rushed to see his new grandson. He was beaming with happiness and he named the baby boy Muhammad. "Muhammad" means "Praised One." This was a name that was hardly ever used among the Arabs, and many people asked him, "Why did you give the boy such an unusual name?" Abdul Muttalib replied, "I know that my grandson will be praised both in this world and in the next."

A Taste of History

From Ibn Hisham's *Sirah:*

"It is recorded that when the mother of Rasulullah ﷺ became pregnant with him she had a vision, and a voice spoke to her, saying, "You are pregnant with the prince of this nation. When he is born on this earth, you must say, 'I place him under the protection of the only One, from the wickedness of every envious person.' And you must name him Muhammad." While she was carrying the child in her womb she saw a light issue from her which illuminated even the castles of Busra in Syria. And Abdullah ibn Abdul Muttalib, the father of the apostle, died while the child was yet unborn.

Rasulullah ﷺ was born on a Monday, on the twelfth day of the month of *Rabi' al-Awwal* in the "Year of the Elephant." At the time of the Prophet's birth a Jewish man standing on the roof of a house in Madinah called for his people. When they assembled around him saying, "What's the matter?" He told them, "Tonight the star has risen under which a prophet is born."

When Amina delivered the baby she sent a message to his grandfather: "A baby is born to you; come and see him." He came and she informed him of what she had seen and heard during her pregnancy and the name she had been ordered to give the child. It is said that his grandfather took the baby boy into the Ka'bah and prayed to Allah ﷻ and thanked Him for His gift; then, he brought him again to his mother."

WE HAVE LEARNED:

- Abraha, the king of Yemen wanted to destroy the Ka'bah with his huge army.
- Allah ﷻ protected the Ka'bah and destroyed the army of Abraha instead.
- Muhammad's father died several months before his birth.
- Muhammad ﷺ was born on Monday, the 12th of *Rabi' al-Awwal*.
- The name "Muhammad" means "Praised One."

WORDS TO KNOW:

Expecting, Fir'awn, Heartbroken, Praise, *Rabi' al-Awwal*

القرآن

QUR'AN CONNECTION:

Let us read what Allah ﷻ says about the "Year of the Elephant" in the Qur'an:

بِسْمِ اللهِ الرَّحْمٰنِ الرَّحِيمِ

أَلَمْ تَرَ كَيْفَ فَعَلَ رَبُّكَ بِأَصْحَبِ الْفِيلِ ۞ أَلَمْ يَجْعَلْ كَيْدَهُمْ فِى تَضْلِيلٍ ۞ وَأَرْسَلَ عَلَيْهِمْ طَيْرًا أَبَابِيلَ ۞ تَرْمِيهِم بِحِجَارَةٍ مِّن سِجِّيلٍ ۞ فَجَعَلَهُمْ كَعَصْفٍ مَّأْكُولٍ ۞

"Have you not seen how your Lord dealt with the companions of the elephant? Did He not bring their plan to nothing? And He sent against them flocks of birds, striking them with stones of baked clay. Then did He make them like a field of stalks and straw which has been eaten up."

(Surah al-Fil 105:1)

18

Muhammad ﷺ moves to the Countryside

Looking Ahead

In this lesson we'll learn about one tradition the Arabs had. They used to send their infants to nurses who lived in the countryside.

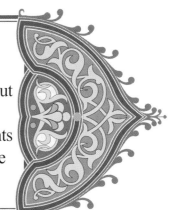

At the time of the birth of Muhammad ﷺ, Makkah had grown to be a big city. It was a center of business where merchants from many countries came to trade.

Makkah also was the most sacred city for the pagan Arabs as they had placed many idols inside the Ka'bah. Every year the people from all over Arabia would come to Makkah to visit the Ka'bah and worship their idols. This made Makkah the most important large city in the region. The traders, visitors and the pilgrims made Makkah a crowded metropolitan city.

The climate of Makkah is a harsh dry desert with very little rainfall. It gets extremely hot during the summer months. Most of the Arab residents of Makkah believed that the crowded, hot environment of Makkah was not healthy for young babies. They also wanted their children to learn the pure Arabic language, the language spoken by the desert *Bedouin* Arabs. They believed that Arabic of the city dwellers became mixed with the visitors and the immigrant non-Arabs.

A traditional Arab village

The villages outside of Makkah were small with no pollution; the air and the water were clean and fresh. Most of the fruits and vegetable were grown by the villagers themselves. The milk from the goats was fresh and healthy. Besides in these villages Arabs spoke a very pure form of the Arabic language.

These advantages convinced most of the rich Arab families to send their babies with the village nurses to be raised with their families during their early childhood.

Even in modern times people who live away from big cities usually have an easier time keeping old customs and traditions. Life in the villages around Makkah was certainly much more difficult, but the people carried on with the very old customs of the Arabs. The villagers spoke a style of Arabic that was especially pure and the people who lived in Makkah wanted their own children to learn the old ways and to spend their childhood in a healthy environment. For that reason, every year village women would come to the city and the *Makkans* would rush to select the best one for their infants.

Aminah wanted to send baby Muhammad ﷺ to live with a woman in a village. She wanted him to grow up healthy and to speak pure Arabic. But she thought that it would be difficult for her to find a nurse since she had lost her husband and did not have enough money to pay.

One day some women of the tribe of Banu Sa'd (also called Banu Hawazin) came to Makkah. They were known for their ability to care for children and their outstanding Arabic language skills. They came to Makkah to find babies who needed nursing. Among them was a woman named Halimah. Many years later the Prophet ﷺ said, "I am the most fluent in Arabic of you all since I belong to the Quraish, and my accent is that of Banu Sa'd."

Halimah was not in good health. She was weak and barely had enough milk to feed her own child. Her camel did not give enough milk either. Her donkey was thin and weak. Because the village people were poor, Halimah hoped to find a child from a rich Quraishi family who could pay her well.

Because Halimah's donkey and camel walked slowly, she could not keep up with the other women of Banu Sa'd, and she arrived in Makkah after them. The other village women had already taken all the babies from the rich Quraishi families. In addition, Halimah looked so worn out that no rich Makkan woman would even think of giving Halimah a baby. She was very sad.

Then Halimah came to know about a baby named Muhammad ﷺ. She went to Aminah's home and talked to both her and Abdul Muttalib, the baby's grandfather. Halimah ﷺ and her husband Harith ﷺ may have been poor, but they were caring people. Aminah made up her mind to send her baby to live with Halimah ﷺ. She was pleased that her baby found a loving family who would care for him and raise him in a healthy environment. But how she would miss him!

Halimah ﷺ was happy to have a baby to care for, even though the pay was not very good. But our Master Muhammad ﷺ proved to be a blessed child. Soon after Halimah ﷺ took him, she found that her breasts were full of milk. She had plenty of milk for both her own baby and for

The Family of Halimah ﷺ

Rasulullah's foster-father's name was Harith ibn 'Abdul 'Uzza. Once Prophet Muhammad ﷺ began to teach Islam to the people of Arabia, Harith ﷺ came to Makkah and embraced Islam along with Halimah ﷺ. Rasulullah ﷺ had one foster-brother named Abdullah and his foster-sisters were Anisa, Hudhaifah and Shaima'. It is reported that Abdullah ﷺ and Shaima ﷺ had accepted Islam. We do not know much more about the two other sisters.

Muhammad ﷺ. Her sickly donkey became strong and her camel started giving plenty of milk.

As he grew, the Blessed Muhammad ﷺ became very popular among the villagers of Banu Sa'd. Allah ﷻ blessed every house he visited. The people were delighted to have such a child among them.

After two years, Halimah ﷺ and her husband took Muhammad ﷺ back to his mother in Makkah, but they were sad to part with him. They asked Aminah if Muhammad ﷺ could stay with them longer. Aminah missed her baby and she wanted to keep him with her. However there was an epidemic in Makkah at that time, so Aminah thought it better for the little boy to live in the village a little longer. So dear little Muhammad ﷺ went back with Halimah and her family.

Halimah's husband was a shepherd who took care of the village's sheep. When Rasulullah ﷺ was old enough, he began to help look after the sheep along with Halimah's children. He would behave as if he was a little shepherd boy. The children loved to play with him.

One day when Rasulullah ﷺ was in the field with Halimah's children, a strange thing happened. Two angels dressed in shimmering white robes came to him. With a diamond knife they opened little Muhammad's chest, removed his heart, rinsed it and then filled it with heavenly *Nur,* or Light. After they did this, they disappeared. All the children saw this and became frightened. They ran home to tell their parents.

When they heard the children's story, Halimah and her husband became frightened as well. They rushed to the field and when they arrived there they found little Muhammad ﷺ sitting and looking up at the sky. He told them what had happened. He pointed up and said, "I saw the angels returning to Heaven."

Halimah ﷺ and her husband were confused. They did not know what all of this meant. But they were happy that little Rasulullah ﷺ wasn't hurt. They decided it was time to take Muhammad ﷺ back to his mother.

Aminah was happy to see her son back home. However, she wanted to know the reason that Halimah and her husband brought young Muhammad ﷺ back to her when they wanted to keep him longer.

Prophet Muhammad ﷺ had great love and respect for his foster-mother Halimah ﷺ and his foster-brothers and sisters and always treated them with great kindness and compassion.

From Ibn Kathir's
as-Sirat an-Nabawiyyah

Sayyidah Halimah 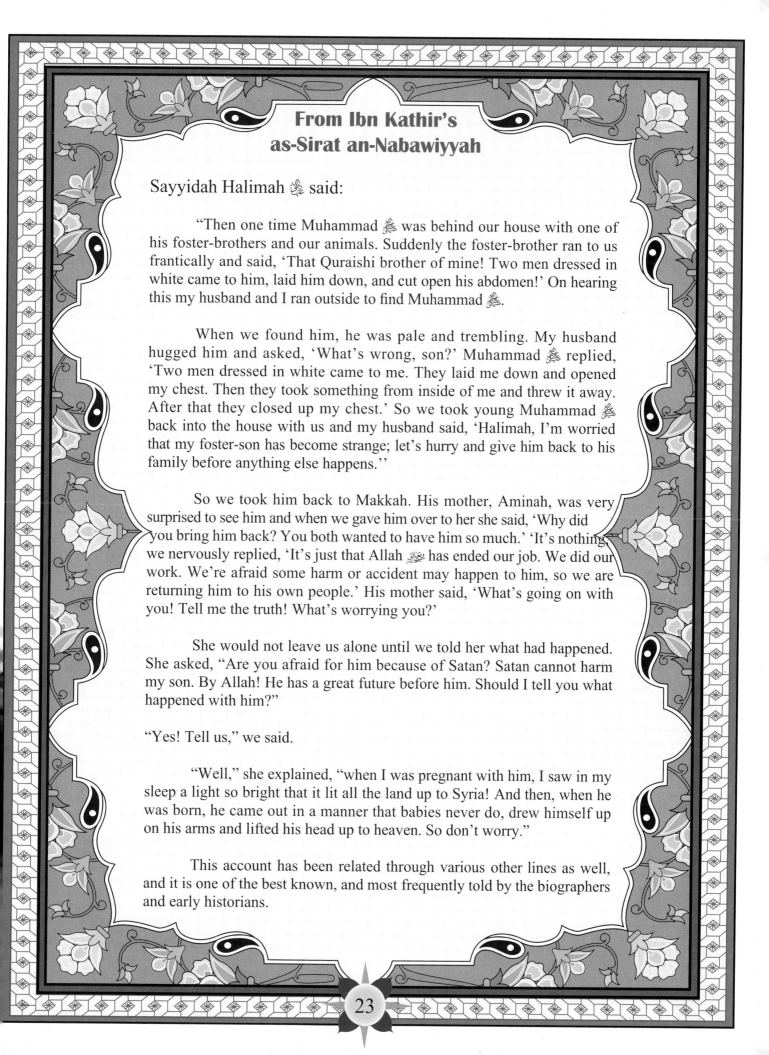 said:

"Then one time Muhammad ﷺ was behind our house with one of his foster-brothers and our animals. Suddenly the foster-brother ran to us frantically and said, 'That Quraishi brother of mine! Two men dressed in white came to him, laid him down, and cut open his abdomen!' On hearing this my husband and I ran outside to find Muhammad ﷺ.

When we found him, he was pale and trembling. My husband hugged him and asked, 'What's wrong, son?' Muhammad ﷺ replied, 'Two men dressed in white came to me. They laid me down and opened my chest. Then they took something from inside of me and threw it away. After that they closed up my chest.' So we took young Muhammad ﷺ back into the house with us and my husband said, 'Halimah, I'm worried that my foster-son has become strange; let's hurry and give him back to his family before anything else happens.''

So we took him back to Makkah. His mother, Aminah, was very surprised to see him and when we gave him over to her she said, 'Why did you bring him back? You both wanted to have him so much.' 'It's nothing,' we nervously replied, 'It's just that Allah ﷻ has ended our job. We did our work. We're afraid some harm or accident may happen to him, so we are returning him to his own people.' His mother said, 'What's going on with you! Tell me the truth! What's worrying you?'

She would not leave us alone until we told her what had happened. She asked, "Are you afraid for him because of Satan? Satan cannot harm my son. By Allah! He has a great future before him. Should I tell you what happened with him?"

"Yes! Tell us," we said.

"Well," she explained, "when I was pregnant with him, I saw in my sleep a light so bright that it lit all the land up to Syria! And then, when he was born, he came out in a manner that babies never do, drew himself up on his arms and lifted his head up to heaven. So don't worry."

This account has been related through various other lines as well, and it is one of the best known, and most frequently told by the biographers and early historians.

WE HAVE LEARNED:

- Muhammad ﷺ went to live with Halimah in her village when he was a baby.
- He was a blessed child.
- Angels opened his heart, washed it, and filled it with Allah's *Nur*.

WORDS TO KNOW:

Banu Sa'd, Environment, Epidemic, Fluent, *Nur*, Shimmer

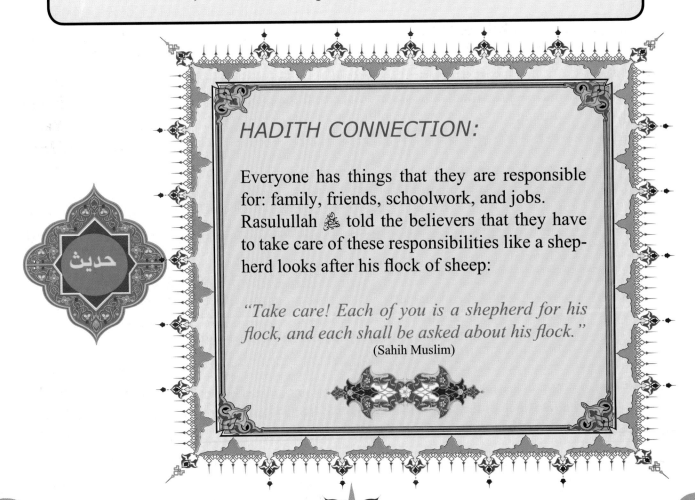

HADITH CONNECTION:

Everyone has things that they are responsible for: family, friends, schoolwork, and jobs. Rasulullah ﷺ told the believers that they have to take care of these responsibilities like a shepherd looks after his flock of sheep:

"Take care! Each of you is a shepherd for his flock, and each shall be asked about his flock."
(Sahih Muslim)

Returning Home

Looking Ahead

Life was hard for Rasulullah ﷺ when he was small. Let's find out why and find out why his grandfather and uncle were so important to him.

Having stayed for a while in the country, little Muhammad ﷺ came back to Makkah to live with his mother. Aminah was very happy. Rasulullah's grandfather, Abdul Muttalib, was also happy. He loved the blessed child dearly for he was a special boy who reminded him of his deceased son, Abdullah.

Abdul Muttalib had many sons, and this meant that Muhammad ﷺ had many uncles. His eldest uncle, Abu Talib, was very fond of him. He cared for Muhammad ﷺ like his own son. His other uncles, Hamza and Abbas, were about his own age. They were his friends, and the three boys always played together. He also had several aunts. Those were happy days for little Muhammad ﷺ. He was surrounded by his loving mother, grandfather, uncles, aunts and cousins.

When Muhammad ﷺ was six years old, Aminah took him on a trip to Yathrib. There, Muhammad ﷺ visited the grave of his father as well as his relatives in the clan of Bani Najjar. They stayed in Yathrib for about a month and then headed back to Makkah.

On the way home, Aminah became very sick and died soon after, at a place called as Al-Abwa', a village seven miles from Yathrib. She was buried there. Muhammad's loving nurse, Barakah, took him back to his grandfather, Abdul Muttalib.

Dear little Muhammad ﷺ! He lost his father before he was born and now his mother was gone too! He loved her so much. He didn't know what to do without her. But he was fortunate to have a loving family waiting for him in Makkah. 'Abdul Muttalib

THINK ABOUT IT!

There are few different narrations of the number of years that Muhammad ﷺ lived with his foster parents. One famous historian named Ibn Ishaq said it was two years, while different historian said it was three years.

Can you think about some of the reasons for the differences in the narration?

Hint: What would happen if your parents and your school forgot to record the date and the day when you started school?

"I will be leaving this life soon," he said. "I want one of you to take Muhammad and raise him."

Hamza came forward and offered himself, but 'Abdul Muttalib told him that because he had no children of his own, he wouldn't know how to be a father. Then Abu Lahab came forward and said he would take care of Muhammad ﷺ. But 'Abdul Muttalib said, "No. You have too many children. You wouldn't be able to give him enough attention." Finally Abu Talib stepped forward. "Father," he said, "I will raise Muhammad in my home." 'Abdul Muttalib agreed that Abu Talib would be the best for little Muhammad ﷺ.

A few days later, 'Abdul Muttalib passed away. Once more Muhammad ﷺ lost a loved one. We can imagine how much he grieved for his grandfather. His loving uncle, Abu Talib, now took care of him. Abu Talib was not wealthy, but he was a very caring man. He looked after Muhammad ﷺ and did everything he could to make his orphaned nephew happy. As a matter of fact he loved Muhammad ﷺ as one of his own sons. Muhammad ﷺ loved his uncle as well. He stayed close to him all the time. He listened to him and respected him.

Muhammad ﷺ had a very friendly character. Everyone loved him and enjoyed his company. He did not fight with other children and he always played fairly. He never used hurtful or rude language. He always spoke the truth. He respected those who were older than him and he

cherished his blessed grandson more than ever. He shared the little boy's grief. The loving grandfather took Muhammad ﷺ in his arms and comforted him. "I will take care of you my child," he said.

From that time on Muhammad ﷺ went to live with his grandfather. 'Abdul Muttalib kept Muhammad ﷺ close to him all the time. He took the boy with him wherever he went.

But it was not long after that 'Abdul Muttalib felt his life coming to an end. He called his sons Hamza, Abu Talib, Abu Lahab and Abbas to his bedside.

was kind to those who were younger than him. People would often tell Abu Talib, "You are lucky to have such a nephew."

There were no schools in Arabia at that time. Very few people knew how to read or write. Since Abu Talib could not afford a teacher for Muhammad ﷺ, the boy grew up unlettered, meaning he could neither read nor write. Yet, when Muhammad ﷺ became a prophet Allah ﷻ gave him the Heavenly Book, the Qur'an. This unlettered and orphaned boy grew to become the greatest personality in the history of the humankind.

WE HAVE LEARNED:

- Muhammad ﷺ went to live with his mother when he was five.
- Aminah died when Muhammad ﷺ was six years old and his grandfather, 'Abdul Muttalib, died when he was eight.
- After that, his uncle, Abu Talib, took care of Muhammad ﷺ.

WORDS TO KNOW:

Character, Deceased, Respect, Unlettered

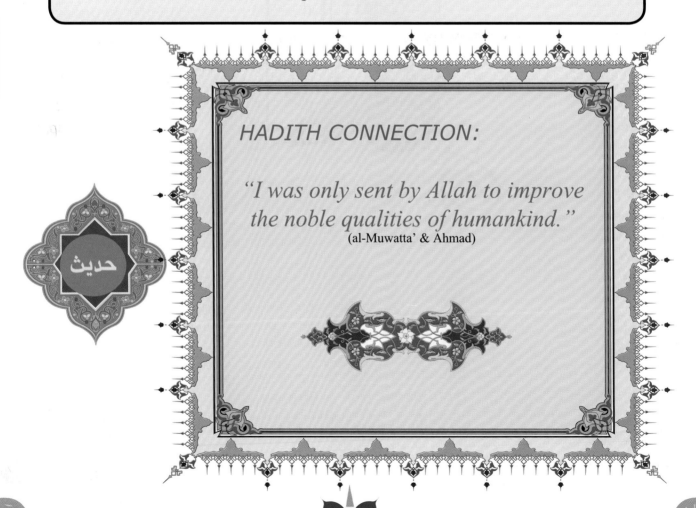

HADITH CONNECTION:

"I was only sent by Allah to improve the noble qualities of humankind."
(al-Muwatta' & Ahmad)

حديث

Muhammad ﷺ: the Peacemaker

Looking Ahead

How did people get along in Arabia before the coming of Islam? Why do you think Rasulullah ﷺ respected the Treaty of Fudul throughout his life?

Muhammad ﷺ grew up happily in his uncle's home. He was surrounded by his young cousins, uncles and aunts. He had many friends but he never participated in activities that were rough or mischievous.

Young Muhammad ﷺ never took part in the worship of the many gods and goddesses of the Arabs. Even though his family often asked him to pray to the idols of the Ka'bah, he always politely refused.

When Muhammad ﷺ was 15 years old, a bloody conflict broke out. Two men from different tribes had an argument, and one of the men killed the other. This started a bloody feud between the two tribes. The fight spread to involve other tribes (including the Quraish), and it became known as the War of Fijar.

Young Muhammad ﷺ went to one battlefield with the Quraish, but he did not take part in the fighting. In fact, it upset him that people fought each other, and he wanted the war stopped. He was unhappy to see all the bloodshed.

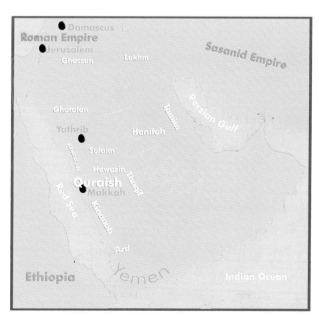

The Arabs were divided into many tribes. These tribes often fought against one another.

After four years of fighting the war finally came to an end. The Quraish wanted all the tribes to have good relations with each other so they came up with a pact, or agreement, that everyone accepted. This pact stated that all the tribes would live in peace and that people should help the poor and the needy. It came to be called the Pact of Fudul. This treaty made Muhammad ﷺ very happy. Many years after he had become a prophet, he said, "I still agree to this pact. It is dearer to me than the most valuable things in this world."

The Pact of Fudul made Makkah a city of peace. All of the Arab tribes respected the Quraish even more than before. At that moment, no one could even think of fighting the Quraish. The Quraish sent their trading caravans to other lands, and no one robbed or harmed them on the way. They did well in business and many of them became very rich.

THE HILF UL-FUDUL

The Messenger of Allah ﷺ was present at the Hilf al-Fudul. This was the most renowned alliance ever heard of in Arabia. It was formed because a man from the town of Zabid, Yemen, had arrived in Makkah with some merchandise and al-As ibn Wa'il, one of the Quraish nobles, bought goods from him and then withheld payment. The Zabidi asked the Quraish nobles for help against al-As ibn Wa'il, but they refused to intervene because of his position. The Zabidi then appealed to the people of Makkah as a whole for support.

All the fair-minded young men were full of enthusiasm to put the matter right. They met in the house of Abdullah ibn Jud'an who prepared food for them. They made a covenant by Allah ﷻ that they would unite with the wronged man against the one who had wronged him until the matter was settled. The Arabs called this pact Hilf al-Fudul, 'The Alliance of Excellence'. They said, 'These people have entered into a state of excellence.' Then they went to al-As ibn Wa'il and took from him what he owed to the Zabidi and handed it over.

The Messenger of Allah ﷺ was proud of this alliance. He held it in such high esteem that after receiving the message of Islam, he said, 'In the house of Abdullah ibn Jud'an I was present at an alliance which was such that if I was invited to take part in it now in Islam, I would still do so.' The Quraish pledged to restore to everyone what was their due and not to allow any aggressor to get the better of those he had wronged.

(from *The Last Prophet* by Sayyed Abul Hassan Ali Nadwi)

WE HAVE LEARNED:

- Prophet Muhammad did not like the War of Fijar.
- He was pleased with the Treaty of Fudul.
- Years later Rasulullah ﷺ said, "I still accept that treaty."

WORDS TO KNOW:

Caravan, Treaty, Treaty of Fudul, Valuable, War of Fijar

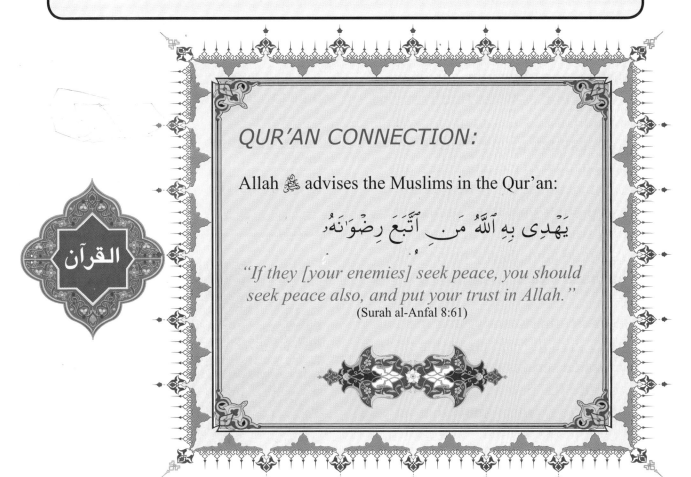

QUR'AN CONNECTION:

Allah ﷻ advises the Muslims in the Qur'an:

يَهْدِى بِهِ ٱللَّهُ مَنِ ٱتَّبَعَ رِضْوَانَهُ

"If they [your enemies] seek peace, you should seek peace also, and put your trust in Allah."
(Surah al-Anfal 8:61)

Muhammad ﷺ Settles an Argument

Lesson 8

Looking Ahead

Rasulullah ﷺ had a noble and just personality long before he was chosen by Allah to carry the message of Islam. What does the event we'll read about in this lesson say about his character?

Young Muhammad ﷺ was known throughout Makkah for his honesty and truthfulness. Instead of calling him Muhammad, people called him as-Sadiq (the Truthful) or al-Amin (the Trustworthy). When he said something, people believed him without a shadow of a doubt. They trusted him so much that they often left their money and other valuables in his care when they went on trips. They knew that no harm would come to any property left in Muhammad's care.

One day when he was a young man, it rained very hard in Makkah, so much so that it caused a serious flood. The waters damaged the Ka'bah and many other buildings. The Quraish knew that they had to rebuild the Ka'bah. Taking part in its rebuilding was considered a great honor and the families of the Quraish tribe divided up the work.

Work began quickly, and soon all of the stones that made up the walls of the Ka'bah were set in place. Now came the time to set the Hajar al-Aswad (the Black Stone). Everyone wanted to have the honor of putting it up, as this was the one of the original stones that Adam ﷺ used to build the very first Ka'bah.

Until modern times, flooding in Makkah had always been a problem whenever the rare heavy rains fell.

32

The Hajar al-Aswad rests in the corner of the Ka'bah. Today it is respectfully encased in a silver frame.

But who would have the honor of placing the Hajar al-Aswad in its place? An argument between all the families broke out. It was certain that unless this dispute was settled fighting would occur.

For four days the Quraish quarreled and bickered among themselves. On the fifth day, a wise old man suggested, "Let us wait until morning. We will gather at the Ka'bah. Then the first person who enters the *Haram,* the holy area around the Ka'bah, after us will decide what to do with the Hajar al-Aswad." Everyone agreed to this suggestion.

Early the next morning, the chiefs of the families and clans gathered at the Haram to see who would be the first to arrive. Soon after, Muhammad ﷺ came to the Ka'bah to pray. Everyone was happy to see him. "Here comes as-Sadiq!" they said eagerly. "Here comes al-Amin!" They knew that there could be no better person for this job than Muhammad ﷺ. He would certainly be a fair judge. He would do what was right and would bring peace.

They explained the problem to Muhammad ﷺ. He listened carefully and then said,

"Let each family select a representative."

THINK ABOUT IT!

What were some of the special characteristics of Muhammad ﷺ that made people accept him as their leader?

As the leader of your school community what special characteristics do you aspire to acquire?

Why?

Write your answers on a separate piece of paper.

The chiefs did what Muhammad ﷺ asked. He then spread his own woolen cloak on the ground and placed the Hajar al-Aswad on it. He asked all of the men to take hold of the cloak and lift it up together. When the cloak had been lifted high enough, Muhammad ﷺ climbed up and put the stone in its place.

Everyone approved of his way of settling the argument. Everyone respected his decision. All of the families were satisfied. They were happy because they had shared in the honor of putting Hajar al-Aswad in its place.

WE HAVE LEARNED:

- People called Muhammad ﷺ as-Sadiq and al-Amin.
- As a young man Muhammad ﷺ was a fair judge.
- Everyone liked his decision about the Black Stone.

WORDS TO KNOW:

al-Amin, Cloak, Hajar al-Aswad, *Haram*, *as-Sadiq*, Satisfied

QUR'AN CONNECTION:

القرآن

Allah advises the Muslims in the Qur'an:

يَهْدِى بِهِ ٱللَّهُ مَنِ ٱتَّبَعَ رِضْوَٰنَهُۥ
سُبُلَ ٱلسَّلَٰمِ وَيُخْرِجُهُم مِّنَ ٱلظُّلُمَٰتِ إِلَى ٱلنُّورِ بِإِذْنِهِۦ
وَيَهْدِيهِمْ إِلَىٰ صِرَٰطٍ مُّسْتَقِيمٍ ﴿١٦﴾

"With it Allah guides him who will follow His pleasure into the ways of peace and brings them out of complete darkness into light by His will and guides them to the right path."

(Surah Ma'idah 5:16)

34

A Trip to Syria

9 Lesson

Looking Ahead

As a young man, the Prophet ﷺ was exposed to the world beyond Arabia. Let's find out what he discovered on his trip to Syria.

Like many of the Quraish, Muhammad's loving uncle, Abu Talib, was a merchant. He had several children and was not wealthy. Muhammad ﷺ wished to help his uncle take care of the family. Abu Talib pleased Muhammad ﷺ by agreeing to his help.

As a merchant, Abu Talib often took merchandise to other towns and cities. To help out, Muhammad ﷺ went with his uncle on these trips. For as long as anyone could remember Arab merchants would travel in caravans, with their camels loaded with goods. They carried their merchandise from place to place on the backs of these animals.

One day, when he was between 11 and 12 years-old, Abu Talib asked young Muhammad ﷺ if he would accompany

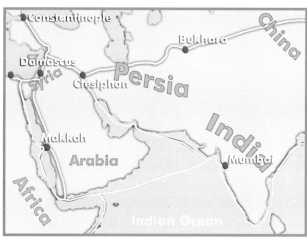

Trade was one way that cultures and civilizations interacted with each other. As you can see from the map, Arabia held an important location in the world's trade routes.

him on the 800 mile journey to Syria. Muhammad ﷺ agreed, and the caravan was gathered for the trip. For many weeks the caravan made its way through the desert. It stopped at all the towns along the way as it journeyed north. Finally, after nearly two months of travel, Muhammad ﷺ, his uncle and their caravan reached a small town called Busra on the very border of Syria.

On the edge of the town lived a Christian monk named Bahira. A monk is a man who gives up the things of this world, stays poor and unmarried and devotes his life to worship. The day Muhammad ﷺ and the caravan arrived, Bahira looked out of the window of his small hut at the vast desert that lay to the south. He saw a caravan approaching, which was certainly nothing unusual. But above it he noticed a single white cloud. Bahira thought it strange that the cloud seemed to follow the caravan, protecting it from the brutally hot sun.

Bahira watched as the caravan drew nearer and then stopped beneath some trees. As soon as everyone was in the shade the cloud disappeared. He was amazed at this and knew that these people must be special. He went to greet the merchants and asked them to join him for lunch. He asked them questions about themselves, looking to see if any of them were especially religious. He did not get the answers he wanted.

Finally he said, "Is everyone from your caravan sitting here with us?" "No," replied Abu Talib. "My nephew is watching the camels. He's young, so we left him there." "No!" said Bahira, "Let me speak with him."

Bahira talked to young Muhammad ﷺ, learning all he could about him. He became sure that Muhammad was a special young man. Bahira decided to try one last test. He asked the child to make a promise by the goddesses of the Arabs, al-Lat and 'Uzza. Muhammad ﷺ refused to do this.

THINK ABOUT IT!

Why did young Muhammad ﷺ not make the promise by the goddesses of the Arabs?

"This boy will become great one day," Bahira said to Abu Talib. "Take him back to your land and look after him." As soon as he had finished trading in Busra, Abu Talib took his nephew back to Makkah. He looked after the boy until he grew up. In time, Muhammad ﷺ became a merchant like Abu Talib. But he had no money of his own. The *Makkans* knew he was as-Sadiq and al-Amin. They trusted his honesty and accepted his word. Rich *Makkans* gave him their money or their goods to do business for them. Muhammad ﷺ worked hard and shared the profits honestly. He became known as an honest, hard working, and successful merchant.

WE HAVE LEARNED:

- Muhammad ﷺ went with Abu Talib on his trading trips.
- A monk named Buhaira told Abu Talib that Muhammad ﷺ would become a great person one day.
- The *Makkans* trusted Muhammad's honesty and gave him their money for business.

WORDS TO KNOW:

Christian, Earnings, Monk, Merchandise, Syria

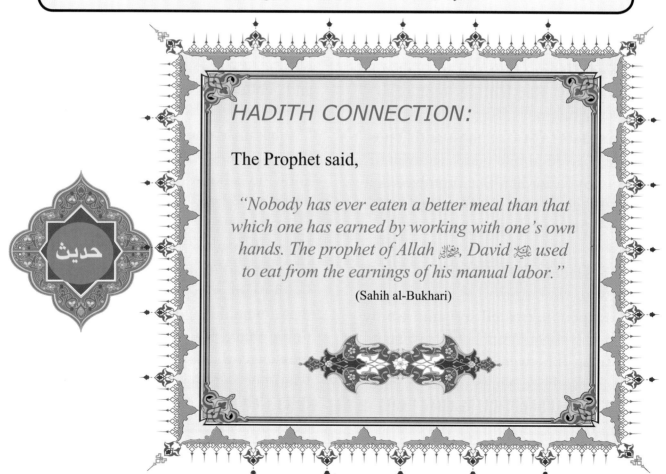

HADITH CONNECTION:

The Prophet said,

"Nobody has ever eaten a better meal than that which one has earned by working with one's own hands. The prophet of Allah ﷻ, David ﷺ used to eat from the earnings of his manual labor."

(Sahih al-Bukhari)

Marriage to Khadijah

Lesson 10

Looking Ahead

Allah ﷻ tells us in Surah Rum, *Ayah* 21 that He places special 'love and mercy' in the hearts of husbands and wives. Let's read about the love between Rasulullah ﷺ and his wife Khadijah ﷺ

A wealthy widow named Khadijah ﷺ, lived in Makkah. Her husband had died many years before. She was a beautiful and kind lady. She lent her money to others for business. She heard of Muhammad's trustworthiness and honesty, so she asked him to take a caravan of goods to Syria for her. She promised that she would give him a double share in the profits. Muhammad ﷺ agreed.

Khadijah sent her trusted servant, Maisarah, along with Muhammad ﷺ. Although very few people treated servants kindly in those days, Muhammad ﷺ respected Maisarah as if he were his own brother. Maisarah watched Muhammad ﷺ carefully. He found him kind, just and truthful.

Muhammad ﷺ sold Khadijah's merchandise and bought other goods with the money for her to sell in Makkah. He returned home and Khadijah was very pleased. Maisarah also told her how kind and gentle Muhammad ﷺ was.

"Muhammad does good business because his customers trust him," he said. "They know he is honest and truthful and does not cheat."

Khadijah was very impressed by Muhammad's character. The respect she felt for him grew into love. She decided that it would be good to marry such a noble man. So soon after, she sent a messenger to Muhammad ﷺ asking if he would be her husband. Muhammad ﷺ discussed this with his uncle Abu Talib. They both agreed that it would be a good match. The two then went to discuss the matter with Khadijah's uncle. All of those involved agreed that this would be a good marriage.

Allah blessed the marriage of Muhammad ﷺ and Khadijah. They lived happily together for 25 years. They had six children together: two sons and four daughters.

Their first child was a boy named al-Qasim. Sadly al-Qasim died when he was very young. Their next children were all daughters: Zainab, Ruqayyah, Umm Kulthum, and finally, Fatimah. Muhammad ﷺ and Khadijah had one more child, a boy named Abdullah, also called Tahir or Tayyib, who died when he was still a baby.

The death of their sons made Rasulullah ﷺ

and Khadijah very sad. But they were very patient and thankful to Allah ﷻ for giving them beautiful and noble children. Rasulullah's daughters grew up to be noble ladies. They all accepted Islam and followed the teachings of their father.

Muhammad ﷺ loved all of his children very much. He especially loved his youngest daughter Fatimah. She was a pious young lady. Rasulullah ﷺ called her the "leader of the young ladies of Paradise." When she grew up, Fatimah married 'Ali, Rasulullah's cousin. 'Ali and Fatimah had two sons together: Hasan and Husain. They also had two daughters, Umm Kulthum and Zainab. Their grandfather, the Prophet Muhammad ﷺ, loved them very much.

THE CHILDREN OF RASULULLAH ﷺ & KHADIJAH ﵂

Rasulullah ﷺ and Khadijah ﵂ had four daughters named:
 Ruqayyah, Umm Kulthum Zainab and Fatimah

According to one tradition he had two sons Al-Qasim, and Abdullah (who was also called Al-Tahir and Al-Tayyib)

Rasulullah ﷺ was also known by his *Kuniyah* Abu al-Qasim. His sons died when small, but his daughters lived to adulthood and grew up as muslim.

WE HAVE LEARNED:

- Maisarah found Muhammad ﷺ to be kind, just and truthful.
- Khadijah ؓ proposed to Muhammad ﷺ and they were married.
- They had six children. Fatimah, their youngest daughter, was the mother of Hasan, Husain, Umm Kulthum and Zainab.

WORDS TO KNOW:

Profits, Pious, Maisarah

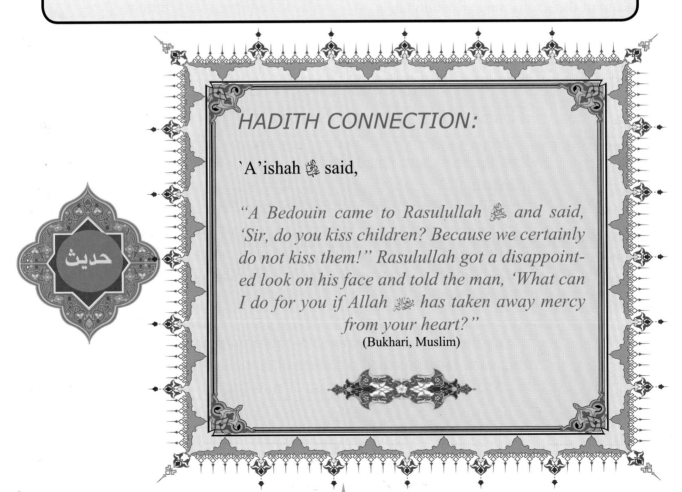

HADITH CONNECTION:

`A'ishah ؓ said,

"A Bedouin came to Rasulullah ﷺ and said, 'Sir, do you kiss children? Because we certainly do not kiss them!" Rasulullah got a disappointed look on his face and told the man, 'What can I do for you if Allah ﷻ has taken away mercy from your heart?"

(Bukhari, Muslim)

The Beginning of Prophethood

Lesson 11

Looking Ahead

Muhammad ﷺ was not interested in the way those in his society behaved. He knew there had to be something more to life than money fame and entertainment..

Muhammad's marriage to Khadijah ﷺ made him rich. He no longer had to struggle to survive. In fact, he could have become even wealthier by continuing in business after his marriage. But Muhammad ﷺ was not interested in making money. He was concerned with other things, like helping others. For instance, Khadijah ﷺ had given Muhammad ﷺ a young slave named Zaid ibn Harith ﷺ. Instead of keeping him as a servant, Muhammad ﷺ freed Zaid and cared for him as if he were his own son. Zaid ﷺ loved his new master so much that he never left him, even after he was freed.

At that time there were only a few Arabs who believed in one God, Allah ﷻ. Muhammad ﷺ was one of those people. He worshipped only Allah ﷻ and did not worship idols. He was unhappy about the ways of his people and their belief in many gods and goddesses.

Slowly Muhammad ﷺ lost interest in business and in making money. He gave away much of his wealth to the poor. It is also said that Rasulullah ﷺ began to experience true dreams. Whatever he would see in his dream at night would come true in real life. He became more comforted by being alone and pondering over the Creator of the universe.

When Muhammad ﷺ would go out of the city towards the valleys around Makkah and pass by the stones and bushes, they would greet him, whispering *"As-Salamu 'Alaikum, Ya Rasulullah! Peace be upon you, O Messenger of Allah!"* When he looked around to find out who was greeting him, he could not find any one.

41

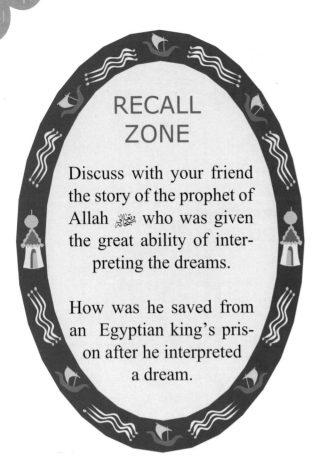

RECALL ZONE

Discuss with your friend the story of the prophet of Allah ﷻ who was given the great ability of interpreting the dreams.

How was he saved from an Egyptian king's prison after he interpreted a dream.

This is the mountain that has the honor of having the most well-known cave in the world-the Cave Hira.

Hira is a small cave about 3.5 meters long and a little over 1.5 meters wide. It is a bright cave with lots of sunshine during the day. The height of the cave is barely enough for a person to stand up.

The Mountain of Light just outside of Makkah.

These strange events continued until one Ramadan, when he received *Wahi*, or revelation, from Allah ﷻ.

Muhammad ﷺ wanted to stay away from the cruelty and badness that was around him as much as he could. He started going to a cave called Hira. The cave was outside Makkah on the top of a tall mountain that is now called the Mountain of Light or the Jabal an-Nur. It was not an easy place to reach, but it was a quiet and peaceful place. Muhammad ﷺ sometimes stayed there for many days thinking about the Creator and praying to Him.

The Mountain of Light is on the north east side of the city of Makkah. It is only about two miles away from Makkah.

It was here in the Cave Hira that Muhammad ﷺ received his first divine revelation. Scholars disagree on the exact date of this event. But most say it was sometime between the 21st and 27th of Ramadan in the year 611 CE.

Khadijah ﷺ loved Muhammad ﷺ dearly. She understood that her husband needed to be alone to worship the one God. She did her best to support him. If Muhammad ﷺ was away at the cave for several days, Khadijah ﷺ would climb the mountain, sometimes with their daughters, taking food for him so he could stay longer. Muhammad ﷺ thanked Allah ﷻ for such a loving wife.

WE HAVE LEARNED:

- ๑ Muhammad ﷺ was not interested in being wealthy.
- ๑ Muhammad ﷺ needed a quiet place to think and to worship Allah ﷻ.
- ๑ He began to go to the cave of Hira and think about Allah ﷻ.
- ๑ Khadijah رضي الله عنها loved her husband and understood his needs.

WORDS TO KNOW:

Hira, Immorality, Zaid ibn Harith رضي الله عنه, Servant, *Wahi*

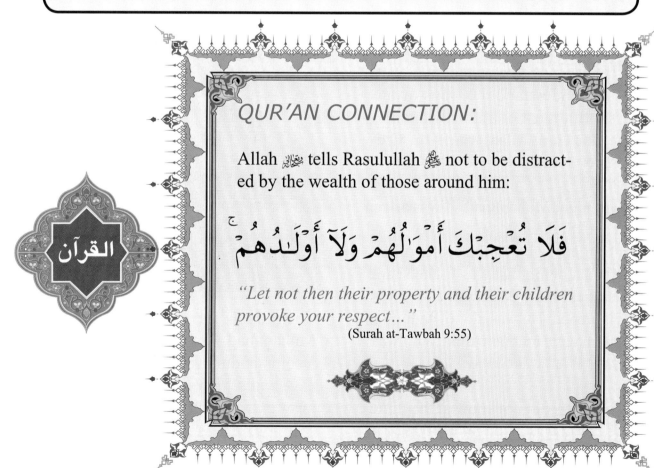

QUR'AN CONNECTION:

Allah ﷻ tells Rasulullah ﷺ not to be distracted by the wealth of those around him:

فَلَا تُعْجِبْكَ أَمْوَالُهُمْ وَلَآ أَوْلَٰدُهُمْ

"Let not then their property and their children provoke your respect..."
(Surah at-Tawbah 9:55)

القرآن

Allah's Last Prophet and Messenger

Looking Ahead

Angel Jibril ﷺ brought *Wahi* to Muhammad ﷺ in the Cave of Hira'. This was the beginning of his mission as Allah's last prophet.

Muhammad ﷺ was now 40 years old, and he spent more and more time in Cave Hira'. He wanted to know the truth about life and to understand the ways of the universe. But most of all, he wanted to find the One God, Allah, who is the Creator of everything.

One calm night Muhammad ﷺ was asleep in the cave. Suddenly, the cave was filled with a brilliant light. At the center of this light stood a being that was in the shape of a beautiful man. Muhammad ﷺ was very frightened. He was alone, high up in a mountain cave and now this! Who was this being? What was happening?

Muhammad ﷺ did not know at that time that the being was an angel called Jibril ﷺ. He was a special angel. Whenever Allah ﷻ sent messages to the prophets,

He sent them through the Angel Jibril ﷺ.

The Angel Jibril ﷺ moved close to Muhammad ﷺ. "Read!" Jibril ﷺ said in a commanding voice that echoed off the cave walls. "I do not know how to read," answered Muhammad ﷺ. Jibril ﷺ moved still closer and grabbed hold of Muhammad ﷺ. "Read!" he said again. "But I do not know how to read!"

Muhammad ﷺ repeated, full of panic. By now Muhammad ﷺ found himself being held by the angel. Jibril pulled him close, so close that Muhammad ﷺ thought his ribs would crack. He was now ready to receive Allah's message. Jibril عليه السلام began to speak the words that Allah سبحانه وتعالى had given him:

اقْرَأْ بِاسْمِ رَبِّكَ الَّذِى خَلَقَ ۝
خَلَقَ الْإِنسَـٰنَ مِنْ عَلَقٍ ۝
اقْرَأْ وَرَبُّكَ الْأَكْرَمُ ۝
الَّذِى عَلَّمَ بِالْقَلَمِ ۝
عَلَّمَ الْإِنسَـٰنَ مَا لَمْ يَعْلَمْ ۝

*"Read in the name of your Lord
Who created,
Created man from a clot of blood.
Read! And your Lord is
the most generous.
The One who taught with the pen.
He taught man what he
did not know."*

(Surah al-Alaq 1-5)

When Jibril عليه السلام stopped speaking, Muhammad ﷺ remembered every word. But he did not know that the angel's words were a revelation from Allah سبحانه وتعالى. The verses Jibril عليه السلام had brought were, in fact, the very first words of the Qur'an. The revelation to prophets is called *Wahi*.

Having delivered the first *Wahi*, Jibril عليه السلام left. When Prophet Muhammad ﷺ came

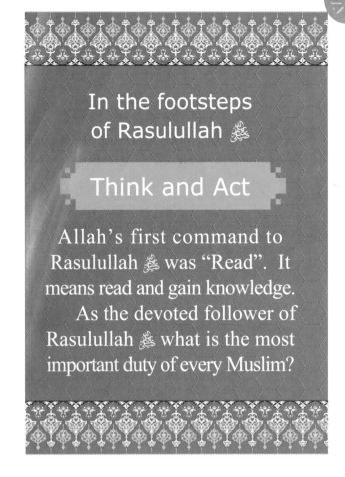

Think and Act

Allah's first command to Rasulullah ﷺ was "Read". It means read and gain knowledge. As the devoted follower of Rasulullah ﷺ what is the most important duty of every Muslim?

out of the cave and reached the middle of the mountain, he heard a voice that was telling him "O Muhammad! You are Allah's Messenger and I am Jibril!" Prophet ﷺ later said that he saw Angel Jibril in the form of a man in every direction he looked in the sky.

Muhammad ﷺ had no idea who the shimmering figure was or why he had come. He did not know that the words the figure had spoken were the Words of Allah, the Lord of the universe. He did not know yet that out of all the people on earth Allah سبحانه وتعالى had chosen him to deliver the last message, the Qur'an. He was frightened with the experience and rushed home to his comforting wife, Khadijah رضى الله عنها.

WE HAVE LEARNED:

- Angel Jibril ﷺ brought the first *Wahi* to Muhammad ﷺ in the cave of Hira'.
- The Qur'an is the collection of all *Wahi* from Allah to Muhammad ﷺ.
- Muhammad ﷺ did not know this was the beginning of his mission as Allah's last prophet and messenger.
- Allah ﷻ asked Rasulullah ﷺ to 'read' in His first revelation.

WORDS TO KNOW:

Wahi, Blood clot, Brilliant, Transmit

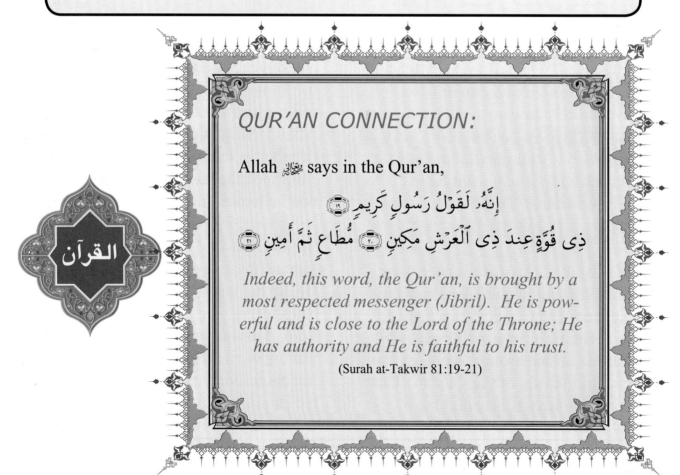

القرآن

QUR'AN CONNECTION:

Allah ﷻ says in the Qur'an,

إِنَّهُ لَقَوْلُ رَسُولٍ كَرِيمٍ ﴿١٩﴾

ذِى قُوَّةٍ عِندَ ذِى ٱلْعَرْشِ مَكِينٍ ﴿٢٠﴾ مُّطَاعٍ ثَمَّ أَمِينٍ ﴿٢١﴾

Indeed, this word, the Qur'an, is brought by a most respected messenger (Jibril). He is powerful and is close to the Lord of the Throne; He has authority and He is faithful to his trust.

(Surah at-Takwir 81:19-21)

Khadijah comforts Muhammad

Looking Ahead

Rasulullah ﷺ was troubled by what had happened in Cave Hira'. We will read about how he found reassurance from his wife.

The strange event that had happened in Cave Hira' made Muhammad ﷺ scared. He didn't know what he had just seen and heard. After Jibril عليه السلام disappeared he left the cave and hurried home. As he was coming down the mountain, he heard the voice of Jibril عليه السلام, "Oh Muhammad! You are the Messenger of God and I am Jibril!" He looked up to see where the voice was coming from and saw the figure of Jibril عليه السلام covering the entire sky! Muhammad ﷺ was terrified by this sight and he rushed home.

When he arrived at his house, he was cold and trembling. "Cover me up! Cover me up!" he said to Khadijah رضى الله عنها. Khadijah رضى الله عنها was very worried when she saw her husband's condition. "What is it? What has happened?" She asked anxiously. Muhammad ﷺ told Khadijah رضى الله عنها about

what he had seen and heard in the cave. Khadijah رضى الله عنها knew her husband's noble character. She knew that the One God of Ibrahim عليه السلام would not let anything bad happen to him. She comforted Muhammad ﷺ saying, "My husband! You are such a good man. You are kind to slaves and to the poor. You love the orphans and comfort widows. You always tell the truth and you keep your promises. Allah عز وجل loves such people. Surely He will never let any harm come to you!" Muhammad ﷺ was comforted by her kind words.

The reassuring words of Khadijah رضى الله عنها made Muhammad ﷺ feel better and less scared. He thanked Allah عز وجل for giving him such a kind, supportive wife.

After comforting Muhammad ﷺ, Khadijah رضى الله عنها went to her elder cousin, Waraqa ibn

THINK ABOUT IT!

Following the tradition of Khadijah ؓ, how do you think a loving wife or husband would comfort their spouse in time of stress, illness or fear?

Nawfal. He was a wise old man who had become a Christian many years before. He was also a very educated man who had studied the holy books of Christianity. Waraqa was known for being a religious and noble man, so Khadijah ؓ spoke to him and told him what had happened to her husband in Cave Hira'.

Waraqa was amazed when he heard this news. He knew that the holy books of the Christians and the Jews predicted the coming of a great prophet and the end of times. He said, "O Khadijah! If you are telling me the truth, then the great angel who visited Musa has now come to your husband. It could be that he is that great prophet whom Allah promised to send."

Then Waraqa continued, "But you must tell him to be steadfast in his belief."

Later, Waraqa met Rasulullah ﷺ at the Ka'bah while he was doing his *Tawwaf* and asked him, "O my friend! Tell me what you have seen and heard." Rasulullah ﷺ told him what had happened in the

cave. Then Waraqa said, "By the Lord in whose hands is my life! You are certainly the *Nabi,* the prophet! Without doubt you have seen the same angel who came to Musa. But the people of Makkah will become your enemies, and they will trouble you. I am very old now and I am sure I won't live much longer. But if I were younger, I would have helped you." Then Waraqa kissed Rasulullah's forehead and the two men parted company.

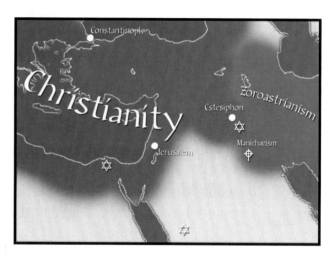

There were two major religions in the Middle East at the time of the coming of Islam. These were Christianity and Zoroastrianism.

The beginning of revelation took place in the month of Ramadan as Allah ﷻ has told us in Surah Baqarah, Ayah 185:

شَهْرُ رَمَضَانَ ٱلَّذِىٓ أُنزِلَ فِيهِ ٱلْقُرْءَانُ هُدًى لِّلنَّاسِ وَبَيِّنَتٍ مِّنَ ٱلْهُدَىٰ وَٱلْفُرْقَانِ

"The month of Ramadan is that in which the Qur'an was revealed, a guidance to humanity and clear proof of the counseling and the criterion..."
(Surah al-Baqara 2:185)

48

A small amount of time passed before Jibril ﷺ visited Sayyidina Muhammad ﷺ again. When Angel Jibril ﷺ visited Rasulullah ﷺ again, he told Rasulullah ﷺ that Allah ﷻ had chosen Muhammad ﷺ to be His last great prophet and messenger.

The Angel Jibril ﷺ recited *Surah Ad-Duha* this time to Prophet Muhammad ﷺ. The verses of *Surah Ad-Duha* told him that he had been chosen as the messenger to mankind. He would be Rasulullah, the Messenger of Allah. Allah told him that He was pleased with him. Through him, Islam would come to all of humanity.

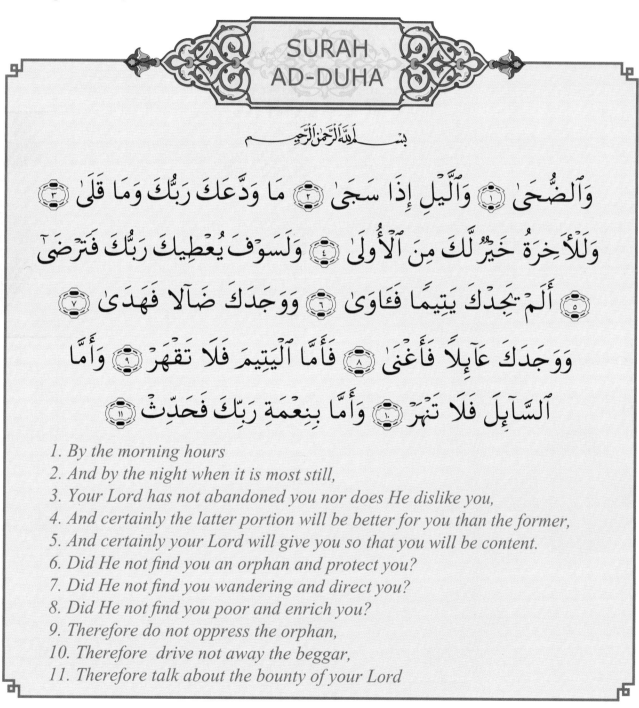

SURAH AD-DUHA

بِسْمِ اللَّهِ الرَّحْمَٰنِ الرَّحِيمِ

وَالضُّحَىٰ ﴿١﴾ وَاللَّيْلِ إِذَا سَجَىٰ ﴿٢﴾ مَا وَدَّعَكَ رَبُّكَ وَمَا قَلَىٰ ﴿٣﴾ وَلَلْآخِرَةُ خَيْرٌ لَّكَ مِنَ الْأُولَىٰ ﴿٤﴾ وَلَسَوْفَ يُعْطِيكَ رَبُّكَ فَتَرْضَىٰ ﴿٥﴾ أَلَمْ يَجِدْكَ يَتِيمًا فَآوَىٰ ﴿٦﴾ وَوَجَدَكَ ضَالًّا فَهَدَىٰ ﴿٧﴾ وَوَجَدَكَ عَائِلًا فَأَغْنَىٰ ﴿٨﴾ فَأَمَّا الْيَتِيمَ فَلَا تَقْهَرْ ﴿٩﴾ وَأَمَّا السَّائِلَ فَلَا تَنْهَرْ ﴿١٠﴾ وَأَمَّا بِنِعْمَةِ رَبِّكَ فَحَدِّثْ ﴿١١﴾

1. By the morning hours
2. And by the night when it is most still,
3. Your Lord has not abandoned you nor does He dislike you,
4. And certainly the latter portion will be better for you than the former,
5. And certainly your Lord will give you so that you will be content.
6. Did He not find you an orphan and protect you?
7. Did He not find you wandering and direct you?
8. Did He not find you poor and enrich you?
9. Therefore do not oppress the orphan,
10. Therefore drive not away the beggar,
11. Therefore talk about the bounty of your Lord

WE HAVE LEARNED:

- Rasulullah ﷺ was troubled by what had happened in Cave Hira', and his wife comforted him.
- Khadijah's cousin, Waraqa ibn Nawfal, told Rasulullah ﷺ he was the prophet promised by Allah in all the previous holy books.
- Sayyidina Muhammad's title was now "Rasulullah."

WORDS TO KNOW:

Christianity, Persecute, Shiver, Abandoned, Content, Bounty

QUR'AN CONNECTION:

In the Qur'an Allah says about Rasulullah ﷺ:

وَمَآ أَرْسَلْنَاكَ إِلَّا كَآفَّةً لِّلنَّاسِ بَشِيرًا وَنَذِيرًا وَلَكِنَّ أَكْثَرَ ٱلنَّاسِ لَا يَعْلَمُونَ ۝

"And We have not sent you except as one who brings good news and a warning for mankind."

(Surah Saba' 34:28)

القرآن

14
Lesson

Looking Ahead

Allah ﷻ instructed Rasulullah ﷺ to invite his family and friends to Islam. Those who believed in him became the first *Sahabah*. Let's read more about this.

Not long after he began to receive *Wahi*, Rasulullah ﷺ was instructed by the angel to invite his family and friends to Islam. The first person to accept Islam was Khadijah, his loving wife. "I know how truthful you are," she said. "If you say this is the truth, I believe you." As a result, the first believer in Rasulullah ﷺ was a woman. Allah ﷻ made the mission of Rasulullah ﷺ easier because of Khadijah ﷺ. Whenever he was sad or troubled by the insults and persecution of the *Kuffar*, she would comfort him and encourage him to remain steadfast in his mission.

'Ali ﷺ was Prophet Muhammad's youthful cousin. He was the young son of Abu Talib. Several years before the *Wahi*, the family of Abu Talib faced difficult times. They found it hard to make a living. To help out Muhammad ﷺ agreed to take young 'Ali to live with him.

When Rasulullah ﷺ began to speak about Allah, 'Ali said, "I know you well. You are an honest man and a loving cousin.

RECALL ZONE!

Ali ﷺ was the cousin of Rasulullah ﷺ and he was also his ----------.

Recall the relationship and write about it on a separate piece of paper.

I believe you." It is said that 'Ali ﷺ was only 10-years-old at that time. The great historian Ibn Ishaq wrote, "When the time for prayer would come, Rasulullah ﷺ would walk out towards the valleys around Makkah and 'Ali ﷺ would accompany him. They would both offer their prayers there and then return home in the evening."

Zaid ibn Haritha ﷺ belonged to the tribe of Banu Kalb, a tribe that lived in southern Syria. He was kidnapped from his family by robbers and slave traders. They sold young Zaid ﷺ to a nephew of Khadijah ﷺ whose name was Hakim ibn Hizam. Hakim gave him to his aunt Khadijah ﷺ, who in turn gave him to Muhammad ﷺ.

Zaid ﷺ came to live in the house of Khadijah ﷺ and Muhammad ﷺ as a young boy. He became very close to Rasulullah ﷺ. Rasulullah ﷺ freed him from slavery. He used to treat him as his son. It is narrated that when Zaid ﷺ heard the message of Islam he became convinced with the words of Rasulullah ﷺ. He loved Rasulullah ﷺ more than he loved his own father. "You were a kind master," he said, "You freed me from slavery and kept me as your own son. I have never heard you tell untruths. Certainly you are a prophet and I believe in you." So Zaid ﷺ became the first young man to accept Islam and offer prayers with Rasulullah ﷺ

Abu Bakr ﷺ was Prophet Muhammad's close friend. They had been companions since they were boys. When the Prophet ﷺ told him about the *Wahi* from Allah ﷻ Abu Bakr ﷺ said, "Everyone trusts you. You have been an excellent friend for as long as I have known you. I have faith in what you say and I believe you are Allah's prophet. I accept Islam." Abu Bakr ﷺ was the first person outside Rasulullah's family to embrace Islam.

In this way the people who were closest to Rasulullah ﷺ and knew him best came to become the first Muslims. How blessed these people were! They spent their time in the company of Rasulullah ﷺ, the last messenger of the Creator. They were often in his company when the *Wahi* came to him. They saw in Rasulullah ﷺ how a perfect human being was supposed to be.

Every Muslim who met Rasulullah ﷺ in person is called, in Arabic, a *Sahabi*, a companion. The plural of *Sahabi* is *Sahabah*. We have already learned that when we hear a male *Sahabi*'s name we should say,

"Radi Allahu 'anhu."

This means "May Allah be pleased with him." For a female companion we say,

"Radi Allahu Anha,"

which means "May Allah be pleased with her." In this book an ﷺ or ﷺ after the name of a *Sahabi* and *Sahabiyah* reminds us to ask for Allah's blessing on that particular *Sahabi*. In this way we ask for Allah's blessings to be on all the *Sahabah* and *Sahabiyah*.

WE HAVE LEARNED:

- Allah ﷾ asked Rasulullah ﷺ to invite his family and friends to Islam.
- Khadijah ﵂, 'Ali, Abu Bakr, and Zaid ﵂ were the first Muslims.
- Saying *"Radi Allahu Ta'ala 'anhu"* after the name of a *Sahabi* reminds us to ask for Allah's blessing on that *Sahabi*.

WORDS TO KNOW:

Sahabah, Sahabi, Sahabiyah, Invite, Plural

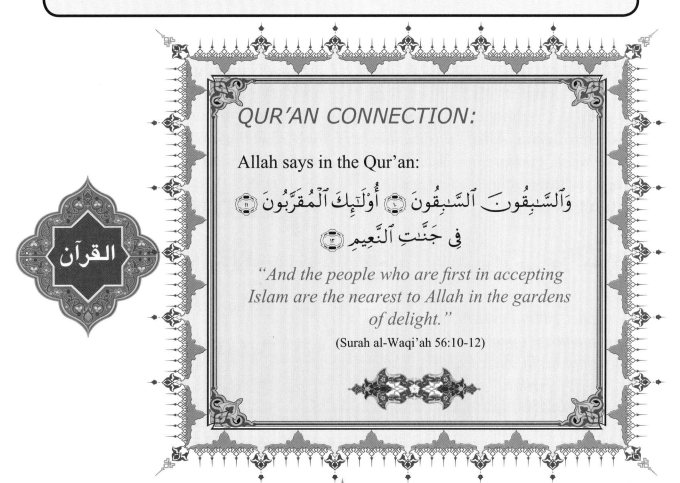

القرآن

QUR'AN CONNECTION:

Allah says in the Qur'an:

وَٱلسَّٰبِقُونَ ٱلسَّٰبِقُونَ ۝ أُوْلَٰٓئِكَ ٱلْمُقَرَّبُونَ ۝ فِى جَنَّٰتِ ٱلنَّعِيمِ ۝

"And the people who are first in accepting Islam are the nearest to Allah in the gardens of delight."

(Surah al-Waqi'ah 56:10-12)

53

Allah's Command to Spread the Message

Looking Ahead

Having invited his family and close friends to Islam, Rasulullah ﷺ now went to the public. We shall read about the response to the message of Islam from the people of Makkah.

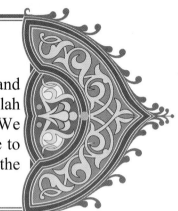

Nearly three years had passed since Rasulullah ﷺ received the first *Wahi* and only a few close family members and friends knew about it. Allah now asked Rasulullah ﷺ to invite all the people of Makkah to Islam. Allah ﷻ sent the following *ayah*, encouraging Rasulullah ﷺ to declare the teachings of His *Din*, Islam, to all the people:

فَٱصْدَعْ بِمَا تُؤْمَرُ وَأَعْرِضْ عَنِ ٱلْمُشْرِكِينَ ﴿٩٤﴾

"(O Prophet!) What ever order is given to you declare it openly and in detail. And turn your sight away from the Mushrikin."
(Surah al-Hijr 15:94)

Rasulullah ﷺ went to a small hill close to the Ka'bah that was called Safa. He stood on the hill and called out for the people of Makkah to gather around him. Since the *Makkans* greatly respected Muhammad ﷺ, they realized that he must have something very important to tell them. They left what they were doing and assembled around Rasulullah ﷺ.

RECALL ZONE!

Who were the *Mushrikin*?

What was wrong with their beliefs?

After he had called the people of Makkah Rasulullah ﷺ stood quietly on the hill. Everyone was waiting to hear what he would say. Then he spoke. "Do you know who I am?" Rasulullah ﷺ asked the *Makkans*. "We certainly do!" they said together in one voice. "You are Muhammad, the son of 'Abdullah. You are one of the noblest of our Quraish tribe."

"Do you trust my words when I speak them?" asked Rasulullah ﷺ.

"Of course we do," they replied, "You are *as-Sadiq* and *al-Amin*."

"Would you believe me if I told you there was an army waiting behind this hill ready to attack you?" Rasulullah ﷺ asked. "Even though you see no army behind this hill?"

"We would believe you," said the people.

"If you would believe me for that, then listen to what I am now going to say," Rasulullah ﷺ continued. "I warn all of you that the Day of Judgment is coming. There is only One God, Allah. None of your many gods and goddesses can do anything. Allah alone is our Creator. It is He Who gave us life and we shall return to Him after death. Then we will be brought back to life, and Allah will judge our good and our bad deeds. So believe in Him alone. Give up your false gods and rude manners and do what is right."

The *Makkans* had never heard anything like this before. They believed in many gods and goddesses, and they certainly did not believe in life after death. For them death meant the end of everything. Because of this, they did not believe that they would be held responsible for what they did in this life. They did not worry much about good and bad since they thought they were free to do whatever they liked, regardless if it hurt themselves or others.

"Is this what you called us here for?" they angrily responded, "Is there something wrong with your mind? You've got to be possessed by *jinns* to talk like this." Their faces grew irritated and angry.

"We've always worshipped our idols," they continued, "And we'll keep on worshipping them. We're not going to believe in what you say!"

One man was particularly annoyed by Rasulullah's words; a man named Abu Lahab. His real name was 'Abdul-'Uzza, but people called him "Abu Lahab" (which meant Father of the Flame) because of his reddish complexion. He was a brother of Abu Talib and of the Prophet's own father, 'Abdullah. He was Rasulullah's uncle!

"You've wasted our time," yelled Abu Lahab angrily as he picked up a small stone and threw it at Rasulullah ﷺ.

Rasulullah ﷺ was upset by the reaction of his people. Yet he received an order from Allah ﷻ to call people to Islam. He had to obey his Lord no matter what.

Over the next weeks and months he kept preaching the Truth to the *Makkans*. Whenever he met people, he told them, "How can a piece of wood or stone be a god? It has no power. It can't do anything for itself or for you. The only God is Allah. You must worry about the Day of Judgment, because the One Who made you will ask you about your beliefs and actions. Nothing can save you from punishment then, except your belief in Allah and your good deeds."

It seemed as if the words of Waraqa were coming true. The rich and powerful *Makkans* started to become very angry with Rasulullah ﷺ. They did not want to hear what he had to say, even though they knew in their hearts he was the most honest man in the city. They only saw that Rasulullah ﷺ was asking everyone to change their beliefs and behavior. Many were afraid that they would lose their power and money if they changed.

Only a few people in Makkah listened to the call of Rasulullah ﷺ and became Muslims. Many of these first Muslims were people who were poor. They did not belong to powerful families. Also among them were slaves, widows, and orphans who had no one to protect them.

Those who did not like what Rasulullah ﷺ said began to persecute those who had become Muslims. These people are called *Kuffar*. They tried to stop others from believing in One God. They called the Muslims awful names and made fun of them. They even began to beat those Muslims who had no one to protect them.

But the believers did not give up. Once a person truly accepts Islam, faith in Allah ﷻ makes him or her very courageous, and these early Muslims had great courage. They stood up against those who wanted to do them harm, even though they were sad to realize that their own people had turned against them.

WE HAVE LEARNED:

- Rasulullah ﷺ invited all the *Makkans* to Islam.
- Abu Lahab, the Prophet's uncle, and other *Makkans* became his enemies.
- Faith in Allah ﷻ made the early Muslims strong and brave.

WORDS TO KNOW:

Assembled , *Mushrikin*, Abu Lahab

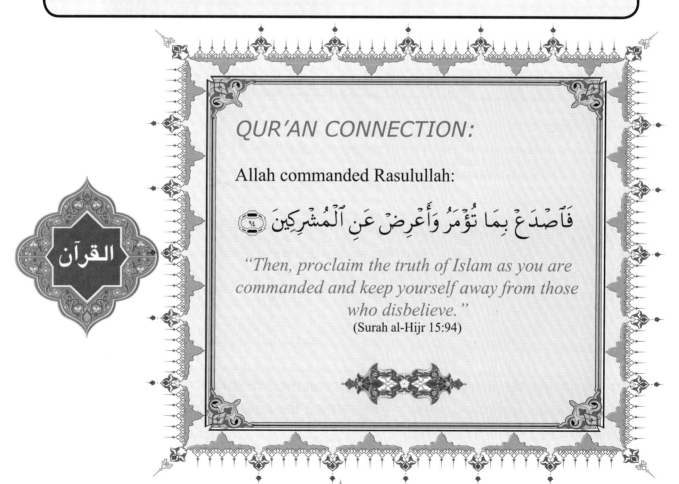

القرآن

QUR'AN CONNECTION:

Allah commanded Rasulullah:

فَٱصْدَعْ بِمَا تُؤْمَرُ وَأَعْرِضْ عَنِ ٱلْمُشْرِكِينَ ۝

"Then, proclaim the truth of Islam as you are commanded and keep yourself away from those who disbelieve."
(Surah al-Hijr 15:94)

THINK ABOUT IT

Look carefully at the following pictures of areas around Safa and Marwa and answer the following questions:

Questions:
1. Look at the two pictures of area around the hills of Safa and Marwa and Compare the changes between 'then' and 'now'.

Location	Then	Now
Area between the two hills.		
Area to the East of the two hills.		
Area to the West of the two hills		

2. Who was the first person to run between the two hills?
3. Name the important pillar of *Hajj* which the *Hujjaj* should perform by walking between the two hills.

The Kuffar go to Abu Talib

The Fourth Year of the Prophethood

Looking Ahead

Those who opposed Islam tried to make Rasulullah ﷺ stop preaching. Let's read about how they tried to stop Islam from spreading.

Rasulullah ﷺ loved and respected his uncle, Abu Talib, a man who had been like a father to him since he was a child. If Abu Talib said something, Muhammad ﷺ always listened with respect. And Abu Talib also felt a deep love for his nephew.

Islam was growing in Makkah day by day.

The *Kuffar* tried to threaten Rasulullah ﷺ with words, but that did not work. They realized that Abu Talib was the only one who could stop Muhammad ﷺ from continuing to preach. They knew that without Abu Talib's protection, Muhammad ﷺ would not be able to speak against their gods or their bad behavior. The *Kuffar* supposed that Rasulullah ﷺ would do

THE PROPHET'S TWO UNCLES (ABU TALIB AND ABU LAHAB)	SAME	DIFFERENT
Blood relation to the Prophet ﷺ		
Treatment of the Prophet ﷺ		
Feelings for the Prophet ﷺ		
Helping the *Kuffar* against the Prophet ﷺ		

anything that his uncle asked him to do. So the chiefs of the *Kuffar* went to speak to Abu Talib about this issue.

"Your nephew is teaching our people a new religion," they said. "He wants us to give up the gods and goddesses of our ancestors. He is turning everything upside down. Please tell him to stop. If he does, we'll give him whatever he wants."

Abu Talib thought about what they said. After the *Kuffar* left, he asked Rasulullah ﷺ to visit him. "My dear nephew," he said, "The chiefs of the Quraish are against you. You can't fight them. Please stop attacking the gods of our ancestors. If you stop, they said they will give you anything you want."

It bothered Rasulullah ﷺ very much to disobey his beloved uncle. But he ﷺ was a prophet, Allah's Messenger, and he was acting under Allah's order.

"I love you deeply uncle," he answered. "But in this matter I cannot obey you. Even if these men put the sun in my right hand and the moon in my left, I cannot stop preaching Islam. I will either complete my work, or I will die trying."

After this conversation, Abu Talib went to the *Kuffar*. "I cannot stop my nephew. His faith in Allah is too strong," said Abu Talib, "But know that I have made a decision to protect him from any harm."

The *Kuffar* were agitated. Their faces became full of rage. What could they do now?

WE HAVE LEARNED:

- ☙ The Quraish chiefs tried to stop Rasulullah ﷺ by speaking to Abu Talib.
- ☙ Rasulullah ﷺ told Abu Talib that in this mattert he could not obey anyone except Allah.
- ☙ Abu Talib told Muhammad ﷺ that he would continue to protect him.

WORDS TO KNOW:

Kuffar, Ancestors, Agitated, Rage

QUR'AN CONNECTION:

Allah asked Muhammad ﷺ in the Qur'an:

القرآن

إِنَّمَآ أُمِرْتُ أَنْ أَعْبُدَ رَبَّ هَـٰذِهِ ٱلْبَلْدَةِ ٱلَّذِى حَرَّمَهَا وَلَهُۥ كُلُّ شَىْءٍ

"O Muhammad, say to the people, I am commanded to obey the Lord of this land which He has made sacred. All things belong to Him…"
(Surah al-Naml 27:91)

An Offer for Rasulullah ﷺ
The Fifth Year of the Prophethood

Looking Ahead

The *Kuffar* offered Rasulullah ﷺ everything he could possibly want if he would stop preaching Islam. In this lesson let's read about what happened next.

Many *Kuffar* could not understand why Muhammad ﷺ was against their gods, since they believed in Allah too. They knew He was the creator of the universe. However they believed that under Him were many gods and goddesses. They also believed that the angels were the daughters of Allah! These beliefs were far away from what Prophet Ibrahim ﷺ had taught them about Allah ﷻ many hundreds of years before.

The *Kuffar* had all kinds of negative thoughts about Rasulullah ﷺ. Some thought he was mentally ill while others thought an evil *jinn* possessed him. Some people thought he was only greedy and wanted money, or that he was after power and wanted to rule over them.

But the *Kuffar* had other worries. The powerful chiefs were especially afraid of the poor and the slaves becoming Muslim. "If they all start following Muhammad, we won't be able to control them," they thought. So they began to use all kinds of threats against Rasulullah ﷺ. But he was not afraid.

One day, the leaders of the *Kuffar* met to discuss this situation. They decided to send a man named 'Utbah ibn Rabi'ah to talk to Rasulullah ﷺ. They wanted to make a deal with him.

"O Muhammad," said 'Utbah. "We have decided to make you an offer. If you stop speaking against our gods and goddesses, we'll give you whatever you want. If you want to be the ruler of Makkah, we'll make you our king. If you want to marry a beautiful woman, we will find the prettiest one for you. If you want wealth, we will make you rich. If you are mentally ill or if evil spirits possess you, we will find a wizard to cure you. We are ready to do anything you want, just stop speaking against our ways."

Rasulullah ﷺ listened politely to 'Utbah's offer. But the offer showed how little the *Kuffar* understood what Rasulullah ﷺ was saying. He recited some verses from the Qur'an about the oneness of Allah ﷻ and the mission of His prophet.

'Utbah finally understood that for Muhammad ﷺ obedience to Allah ﷻ

was the only important thing in life, and nothing could make him give that up. He went back to the chiefs disappointed that the plan did not work.

"Muhammad is not normal," he said to his friends "He does not want wealth or power. His faith in Allah is firm and can't be shaken. We won't be able to change his mind."

The *Kuffar* were furious. They would never leave Muhammad alone as long as he spoke against their beliefs and their behavior. They began thinking about other ways to stop him.

THINK ABOUT IT

OFFERS	Good Deal	Bad deal
The *Kuffar* asked Rasulullah ﷺ to stop teaching Islam and they would make him their king. Do you think it was a ------------		
Abu Talib told the *Kuffar* of Makkah that he would keep supporting his nephew no matter what. Do you think that it was a -----		
The *Kuffar* of Makkah told Rasulullah ﷺ that they would give him a lot of money if he stopped teaching Islam. Rasulullah ﷺ told them that this was a----		
Rasulullah ﷺ told the *Kuffar* that he would not stop talking against their wrong ways and teaching about Allah no matter what they offer him. The *Kuffar* said that it was a ----------		

WE HAVE LEARNED:

- The *Kuffar* offered Rasulullah ﷺ everything he could possibly want if he would stop preaching Islam.
- 'Utbah finally understood that obedience to Allah was the only thing that mattered to Muhammad ﷺ.
- The *Kuffar* were furious and started thinking of other ways to stop Rasulullah ﷺ.

WORDS TO KNOW:

Wealth, Obedience, Furious, Deal, Mentally ill

QUR'AN CONNECTION:

Allah told Rasulullah ﷺ:

قُل مَآ أَسْئَلُكُم عَلَيْهِ مِنْ أَجْرٍ إِلَّا مَن شَآءَ
أَن يَتَّخِذَ إِلَىٰ رَبِّهِۦ سَبِيلًا ۝

"Say, I do not ask for any reward from you for my services. I'm doing this just so that those who want to will follow a path to their Lord."
(Surah al-Furqan 25:57)

القرآن

The Muslims Migrate to Ethiopia

The Fifth Year of the Prophethood

Looking Ahead

When the tortures of the *Kuffar* became too much Rasulullah ﷺ asked a group of Muslims to leave for Africa. We'll read about their journey in this lesson.

Prophet Muhammad ﷺ began to preach everyday. He went wherever there were gatherings to talk about Islam. He would always go to the Ka'bah and call people to Islam. He recited verses of the Qur'an to them. When people listened to the verses, they realized that those words could not be the words of any human being. They had to be the words of the Creator of the universe.

The *Kuffar* continued to oppose Rasulullah ﷺ, but they had no way to stop him since he had Abu Talib's support. But those Muslims who were poor, slaves, orphans or widows who accepted Islam became easy targets for their anger. These people were weak and had no supporters. The *Kuffar* beat some of them very badly, while others were forced to lie down on the burning desert sands. A few of them were even tortured to death.

Yet none of the hardships inflicted by the *Kuffar* could make the Muslims give up their faith. They understood the truth, and they were willing to give up their lives for it rather than go back to their old beliefs. They had faith in Allah's help for those who are steadfast and patient. Although the *Kuffar* did every cruel thing, they could to discourage the Muslims. Not a single one gave up Islam.

As the cruelties of the *Kuffar* became worse, the Prophet ﷺ told some of the believers to leave Makkah. He told them to leave for a land called Ethiopia. A Muslim must migrate to a safe place if he or she is not free to practice Islam in the land where they live.

Ethiopia is a land in East Africa, and it lies across the Red Sea from Arabia. During the time of Rasulullah ﷺ most of the people of that land were Christians. The king of Ethiopia was a just ruler who believed in One God. Because of this belief the Prophet ﷺ hoped that he would protect any Muslim who came to him.

In the dead of night a group of about 16 Muslims slipped away from Makkah, but the *Kuffar* soon learned about their escape. They sent some men to follow the group all the way to Ethiopia. They were not going to let these people get away.

It took the Muslims over a month to cover the 700 miles between Makkah and the palace of the king. When they arrived in the royal city of Axum, they went straight to the king's palace.

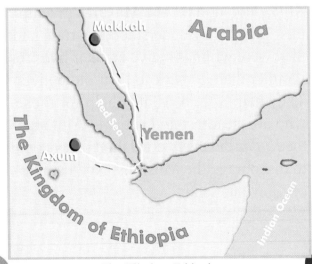

The Hijrah to Ethiopia

While they were waiting to see the king, a group of Makkan *Kuffar* showed up under the leadership of `Amr ibn al-`As. "You will come back with us to Makkah to pay for your disobedience to our ways," he angrily told the Muslims, "I shall tell the king of the trouble you people have caused in our city."

Finally, both groups were allowed into the royal hall where the king received his guests.

"Your Majesty!" said 'Amr to the king. "There is a group from among our people who have run to your land. They follow a religion which nobody has ever heard of. They have refused to follow the religion of our ancestors.

"The chiefs of our city have sent us to ask you to give them back to us," continued 'Amr. "They know what trouble they have caused us."

The king called the Muslims forward and asked them about their religion. Ja'far ibn Abi Talib ﷺ (who was a cousin of the Prophet) was the leader of the group of Muslims. He stepped forward and said, "Your Majesty, we Arabs were an ignorant people, worshipping gods of stone and wood and eating the rotten meat of dead animals. We committed all sorts of shameful acts. We feuded with each other, treated visitors badly, and the strong among us bullied the weak." The king listened closely as Ja'far ﷺ went on, "Our people behaved like this until God sent us a prophet; a man whose truthfulness, trustworthiness and honesty were well-known to everyone. He told us to worship One God alone and not to worship the idols which we and our ancestors used to worship. He told us to speak the truth and to keep our promises. He told us to love our relatives and to be helpful to our neighbors. He told us to avoid killing and using rude language. He told us not to take away an orphan's belongings and to treat women respectfully. We believe in him and what he told us."

"And when we did these good things, O mighty king," Ja'far continued, "our own people attacked us. They tried everything to make us give up our belief and take us back to disgraceful behavior and the worship of idols. They made life awful for us. So we came to your kingdom asking for your protection and hoping to live in peace here."

The king was moved by the words of Ja'far ﷺ. He turned to `Amr ibn al-`As and the *Kuffar*. "Go home," he told them. "And tell your chiefs that these good people are welcome to live peacefully in my kingdom for as long as they wish." Thus, the ruler of Ethiopia offered asylum to the persecuted Muslim refugees from Makkah.

Many countries in the modern world offer asylum to those people who suffer persecution in their own country because of their faith or ideology. Asylum is a form of protection that allows individuals who remain in a country which can protect them from the atrocities of the government or other powerful groups in their own country.

The *Kuffar* were enraged when they heard these words of the king. But there was nothing they could do. The king was very powerful and all they could do was go back to Makkah and tell their leaders their failure to convince the King of Ethiopia.

United Nations High Commissioner for Refugees (UNHCR)

THE UNHCR was established in the late 1940s, soon after the creation of United Nations. It oversees the process of accepting and settling the refugees and asylum seekers in different countries.

The UN's biggest concern at that time was thousands of refugees in Europe who had been driven from their homes during and after World War II and who had no country to protect them. Since then, the number of refugees--as well the countries they are fleeing from-- has increased.

THE UNHCR, based in Geneva, has a worldwide staff of 6,000. In 2008 it had a program budget of over $4 billion. Funds to run the organization come largely from annual voluntary pledges from member countries and also from private donors. The U.S. is by far the largest donor contributing over $300 million per year.

The High Commissioner for Refugees is appointed by the United Nations for five year terms.

WE HAVE LEARNED:

- Many Muslims were persecuted and tortured by the Quraish.
- Some Muslims made Hijra to Ethiopia to seek protection from the Christian king.
- The king protected the Muslims from the Quraish.

WORDS TO KNOW:

Hijra, Disgraceful, Ethiopia, Inflict, Steadfast

القرآن

QUR'AN CONNECTION:

Allah says in the Qur'an:

وَٱلَّذِينَ هَاجَرُواْ فِى ٱللَّهِ مِنۢ بَعْدِ مَا ظُلِمُواْ لَنُبَوِّئَنَّهُمْ فِى ٱلدُّنْيَا حَسَنَةً ۖ وَلَأَجْرُ ٱلْأَخِرَةِ أَكْبَرُ ۚ لَوْ كَانُواْ يَعْلَمُونَ ﴿٤١﴾

"To those who make Hijra for Allah, after they are persecuted, We will secure them well in this world. And the reward of the Hereafter is much greater – if they only knew."

(Surah an-Nahl 16:41)

19 Lesson

Looking Ahead

When the *Kuffar* realized they couldn't stop Rasulullah ﷺ from preaching they decided to take harsh measures against the Muslims in Makkah.

The first Muslims included all kinds of people: rich and poor, men and women. Many were humble people who were not members of powerful families or clans. Some of the Muslims were the slaves of rich chiefs. Their masters often tortured them because of their belief in Islam.

One such man was Bilal ibn Rabah ﷺ. Bilal ﷺ was often called al-Habashi, which is the Arabic word describing the lands of the Horn of Africa. His parents were originally from that area but were taken as slaves to Makkah.

Bilal ﷺ heard the message of Islam and accepted it. However when his master, `Umayyah ibn Khalaf, ordered him to give up the faith, he refused.

This defiance greatly annoyed `Umayyah

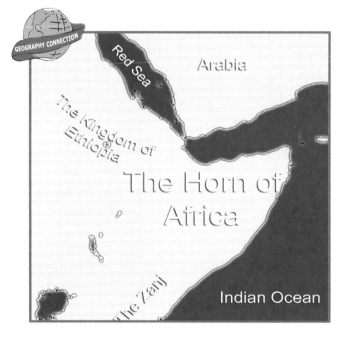

GEOGRAPHY CONNECTION

Red Sea

Arabia

The Kingdom of Ethiopia

The Horn of Africa

The Zanj

Indian Ocean

and to punish Bilal ﷺ he took him out to the desert at midday. He ordered his men to tie Bilal ﷺ down on the blazing sand. Then large stones were placed on his stomach so he couldn't move. "Give up this religion of Muhammad!" `Umayyah yelled. But as Bilal's body was blistered from the heat, all he would say was, "Ahad, Ahad!" (Allah is One! Allah is One!)

Another slave who had embraced Islam was an elderly woman named Zunairah ♦. She was a slave of a particularly wicked man named `Amr ibn Hisham, who later became known as Abu Jahl, "Father of Ignorance." Abu Jahl hated the fact that one of his slaves became Muslim. He started to abuse Zunairah ♦ very badly. He used to whip her every day, but she always said, "Allah is One! Muhammad is Allah's prophet!"

Such words only made Abu Jahl angrier. One day he beat Zunairah ♦ so badly on the head that she became blind. He mocked her and said, "Hah! Look! It is our gods that have made you blind!"

"No! Your idols are blind themselves," Zunairah ♦ answered with tears. "How could they make me blind?" Abu Jahl only laughed and walked away.

Then a miracle happened! When Zunairah ♦ woke up the next morning she discovered that she could see again. But even this did not convince Abu Jahl of Allah's power. "This is only more of Muhammad's trickery!" he scoffed.

Even worse treatment came for Yasir ♦, his wife Sumayyah ♦, and their son 'Ammar ♦. Because they did not have a strong family or clan to protect them, Abu Jahl decided to make an example of them. "Give up this faith," he said, "or you will pay dearly!" When they refused,

THINK ABOUT IT!

Jahl is an Arabic word. It means "ignorance". What do you think were some of the ways that the title "Abu Jahl' the father of the ignorance was suitable for Amr Ibn Hisham?

the family was taken out to the desert and tortured. Yasir ♦ was forced to lie on burning hot rocks and had boiling water poured over him. 'Ammar ♦ and his mother were whipped until they almost bled to death.

The Prophet ﷺ passed by the place where they lay and saw them. He was very distressed to see the family suffering. He told them and said, "Be patient, family of Yasir! We shall meet you in Jannah!"

Eventually Sumayyah ♦, who was an elderly woman, was killed by Abu Jahl and Yasir ♦ died of his wounds. Allah ﷻ ended their difficulties by taking them from this life. He blessed them both with a beautiful home in Jannah as a reward for the patience. Yasir and Sumayyah ♦ were the first martyrs for the cause of Allah ﷻ and His Messenger.

Many Muslims in Makkah suffered from such cruelties. But their love of Allah and His Messenger was great and their faith only grew stronger under such harsh treatment. They gave up their lives, but they never gave up Prophet and the Din he brought. May Allah bless them all with Heaven and give them a great reward!

WE HAVE LEARNED:

- The first Muslims included all kinds of people; rich and poor, men and women.
- Bilal ibn Rabbah ﵁ was persecuted greatly by his master Umayyah ibn Khalf.
- The first martyrs of Islam were Summaiyah ﵂ and her husband Yasir ﵁.
- The love of Allah and His Messenger was so strong in the hearts of first Muslims that they gave up their lives but they never gave up the Prophet ﷺ and the *Din* he brought.

WORDS TO KNOW:

Ahad, Defiance, Habashi, Miracle, Trickery

QUR'AN CONNECTION:

القرآن

Allah says in the Qur'an:

وَلَنَبْلُوَنَّكُم بِشَىْءٍ مِّنَ ٱلْخَوْفِ وَٱلْجُوعِ
وَنَقْصٍ مِّنَ ٱلْأَمْوَٰلِ وَٱلْأَنفُسِ وَٱلثَّمَرَٰتِ ۗ وَبَشِّرِ ٱلصَّٰبِرِينَ ﴿١٥٥﴾
ٱلَّذِينَ إِذَآ أَصَٰبَتْهُم مُّصِيبَةٌ قَالُوٓا۟ إِنَّا لِلَّهِ وَإِنَّآ إِلَيْهِ رَٰجِعُونَ ﴿١٥٦﴾
أُو۟لَٰٓئِكَ عَلَيْهِمْ صَلَوَٰتٌ مِّن رَّبِّهِمْ وَرَحْمَةٌ ۖ
وَأُو۟لَٰٓئِكَ هُمُ ٱلْمُهْتَدُونَ ﴿١٥٧﴾

"And surely We shall test you with fear and hunger, and loss of wealth and life and the fruits of your labor; and give good news to those who are patient, those who say, when misfortune comes to them, 'we belong to Allah and unto Him we will return.' These are the people to whom blessings and mercy come from their Lord. They are the rightly guided."
(Surah al-Baqarah 2:155-157)

The Kuffar Persecute Rasullullah ﷺ

Looking Ahead

Just as they started to torture and kill Muslims, the *Kuffar* began to physically abuse Rasullullah ﷺ. Let's read about what he did in response.

Despite the persecutions, the number of Muslims grew and grew. It made the *Kuffar* furious to see this and they knew that Rasullullah ﷺ was responsible for it. They certainly wanted to kill him, but as long as Abu Talib was there to protect Muhammad ﷺ, the *Kuffar* did not dare to take his life. If they did, war would certainly break out between the clans.

So the *Kuffar* tried different ways to torment the Prophet ﷺ. His uncle, Abu Lahab, was one of the most abusive of the chiefs. He and Abu Jahl would follow Rasullullah ﷺ as he walked through the streets of Makkah. "O people! Say '*la ilaha illa Allah*' and you will be blessed," Rasullullah ﷺ would say. "Don't believe him!" Abu Lahab and Abu Jahl would then cry out, "He's an enemy to our gods! He's a liar! He's

RECALL ZONE!

Recite *Surah* "Lahab' and read its meaning.
Think about what Allah ﷻ is telling us about Abu Lahab and his wife.

a magician! He's crazy!" They would follow this with bad words and insults.

Abu Lahab's wife, Umm Jamil, was even worse than her husband. She wrote nasty and insulting songs about the Prophet ﷺ. At night time when the streets were pitch-black, Umm Jamil scattered sharp, thorny branches in front of Rasulullah's home. Whenever he returned home at night, he would walk on them, and his feet would bleed.

Another time, a man tried to choke Rasulullah ﷺ while he was praying. However Abu Bakr ؓ arrived just in time to rescue him. Sometimes *Kuffar* threw dirt on his head when he was praying or left rotten garbage in front of his door. They often followed him around shouting, "Here comes the crazy man!" Despite all of this, Rasulullah ﷺ never said a mean word back to these people.

There was one woman who collected all the guts and intestines from slaughtered sheep and goats. Then when Rasulullah ﷺ walked down her street on his way to the Ka'bah, she would throw this awful stuff on him.

The treatment of these people made Rasulullah ﷺ sad, but he was sadder because they would not accept the truth. Still, he never spoke angrily to them because he realized they were being tricked by *Shaitan*. He prayed to Allah ﷻ for the patience to bear this suffering, and he asked Allah ﷻ to guide those who hated him and Islam.

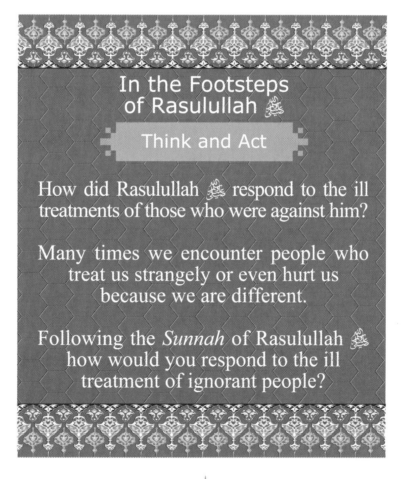

In the Footsteps of Rasulullah ﷺ

Think and Act

How did Rasulullah ﷺ respond to the ill treatments of those who were against him?

Many times we encounter people who treat us strangely or even hurt us because we are different.

Following the *Sunnah* of Rasulullah ﷺ how would you respond to the ill treatment of ignorant people?

WE HAVE LEARNED:

- The *Kuffar* tried to torment and injure Rasulullah ﷺ in many ways.
- Abu Lahab and Abu Jahl were the leaders of the *Kuffar* who tried to hurt Rasulullah.
- Rasulullah ﷺ prayed to Allah ﷻ to give him patience and to guide the *Kuffar*.

WORDS TO KNOW:

Abusive, Intestines, Responsible

QUR'AN CONNECTION:

Read how Abu Lahab and his wife are condemned by Allah in the Qur'an:

بِسۡمِ ٱللَّهِ ٱلرَّحۡمَٰنِ ٱلرَّحِيمِ

تَبَّتۡ يَدَآ أَبِى لَهَبٍ وَتَبَّ ۝ مَآ أَغۡنَىٰ عَنۡهُ مَالُهُۥ وَمَا كَسَبَ ۝ سَيَصۡلَىٰ نَارًا ذَاتَ لَهَبٍ ۝ وَٱمۡرَأَتُهُۥ حَمَّالَةَ ٱلۡحَطَبِ ۝ فِى جِيدِهَا حَبۡلٌ مِّن مَّسَدِۭ ۝

"The power of Abu Lahab will perish and he will himself perish. His wealth and gain will not be able to save him. He shall burn in the flaming fire. And his wife, a carrier of wood, shall have a rope of palm fiber around her neck."

(Surah al-Lahab 111:1-5)

القرآن

74

Hamzah ؓ and 'Umar ؓ Accept Islam

The Sixth Year of the Prophethood

Lesson 21

Looking Ahead

Hamza ؓ and 'Umar ؓ were two important men of the Quraish. Both of them accepted Islam and helped the believers.

Sayyidina Hamza ؓ, one of the uncles of Rasulullah ﷺ, was a brave man who was respected by everyone for his courage. He was also known for being a strong man. Although he was close to the Prophet ﷺ, he had not accepted Islam.

One day Abu Jahl saw Rasulullah ﷺ sitting quietly on the hill of Safa, close to the Ka'bah. When he saw that Rasulullah ﷺ was alone, Abu Jahl ran over and began beating him with his staff. He was calling him all kinds of names. Rasulullah ﷺ remained silent and suffered the abuse.

A lady saw this happening from her window and was upset. When she went outside she saw Hamza ؓ, the Prophet's uncle, coming up the street as he returned from hunting. She ran to him and said, "Your nephew is being beaten and cursed!

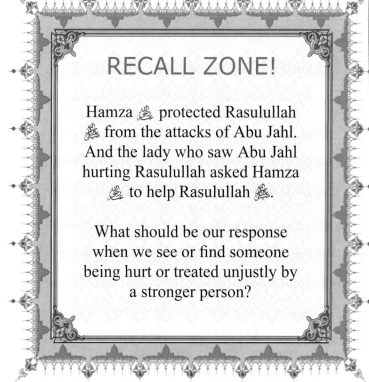

RECALL ZONE!

Hamza ؓ protected Rasulullah ﷺ from the attacks of Abu Jahl. And the lady who saw Abu Jahl hurting Rasulullah asked Hamza ؓ to help Rasulullah ﷺ.

What should be our response when we see or find someone being hurt or treated unjustly by a stronger person?

You must do something!" Hamza ؓ went straight for the Ka'bah and saw Abu Jahl beating Rasulullah ﷺ. With his great strength he hit Abu Jahl on the head with his bow.

"Why don't you try that with me?" Hamza ؓ exclaimed. "I am for my nephew's faith! Fight me if you dare!"

Abu Jahl was afraid of Hamza ؓ and he apologized.

It was his love for his nephew, Muhammad ﷺ, which made Hamza ؓ angry. Suddenly he was filled with the desire to become a Muslim. He went to Rasulullah ﷺ and said, "I believe in you. I believe that there is only One God, and that you are his messenger." Hamza's acceptance of Islam made poor and weak Muslims feel more secure.

Another powerful person in Makkah was Sayyidina `Umar ibn al-Khattab ؓ. Like Hamza, `Umar ؓ was a strong man, who always enjoyed a good fight. Before his heart had changed, `Umar hated Islam so much that one day he made up his mind to take the life of Rasulullah ﷺ. He grabbed his sword and went out to search for him.

On the way, he learned that his sister Fatimah and her husband had become Muslims. He was furious when he heard this and rushed to Fatimah's house where he found her and her husband reading pages from the Qur'an.

`Umar was so angry that he started beating them both. Although his sister was bleeding, neither she nor her husband hit back.

Instead, they kept saying, "`Umar Stop! Stop! We shall not leave Islam even if you kill us! We shall not leave Muhammad!"

`Umar was astonished by their words and devotion. When he saw his sister bleeding, he started feeling sorry for what he had done. He wondered what could make both of them believe so strongly. So he decided to read the Qur'an himself.

"Show me what you were reading when I came in," he said.

"You must wash first, because you have to be pure to touch it," Fatimah said. `Umar did as she told him. He was now very interested in learning about the Qur'an.

Fatimah and her husband recited some verses. 'Umar listened in silence, but his heart beat fast with excitement. He had never heard such words or ideas before. His heart trembled.

"Allahu Akbar!" he exclaimed. "Allah is the greatest." And then he went straight to Rasulullah ﷺ and accepted Islam. As Allah ﷻ willed, one of Islam's worst enemies had now become one of its most faithful friends.

Hamza ؓ and 'Umar ؓ were strong and respected men. Now both of them were ready to fight anyone for the sake of Allah ﷻ and His prophet. They told Rasulullah ﷺ, "The Muslims need no longer be afraid of the *Kuffar*. They can now perform their *Salah* openly."

All Muslims went to the Ka'bah and prayed. The *Kuffar* watched them angrily, but they were afraid to take any action against them.

LET US LEARN SOME FACTS ABOUT ANGER

Anger is an emotional response to a grievance. It may be a real grievance or imaginary one. Anger, if uncontrolled leads to violence. It affects our physical and emotional state. Some physical signs of anger include: Heightened blood pressure; increased stress, shortness of breath; heart palpitations; trembling; increased physical strength; speech and movements are much faster and intense.

It is important to understand the ill effects of being angry on our thoughts and actions. All of the great religions of the world criticize the act of being angry.

"Do not let the sun go down on your anger."
(The New Testament)

"You will not be punished for your anger; you will be punished by your anger."
(the Buddha)

"The strong is not the one who overcomes the people by his strength, but the strong is one who controls himself while in anger."
(Rasulullah ﷺ)

It is narrated in Bukhari that "two Muslims were arguing in the presence of Rasulullah ﷺ. One of them became so angry that his face went red and his veins swelled. Rasulullah ﷺ lifted his face toward that person and said to him that, 'I know a sentence if you were to say it your anger will go away. The sentence is this:

$$أَعُوذُ بِاللَّهِ مِنَ الشَّيْطَانِ الرَّجِيمِ$$

"I seek Allah's protection from the cursed Shaitan"

WHAT WOULD YOU DO?
In the light of the above information about anger, what will you do when you feel angry?

WE HAVE LEARNED:

- Sayyidina Hamza ﷺ and Sayyidina 'Umar ﷺ were two strong, brave men of the Quraish.
- Both of them accepted Islam.
- After that, the Muslims were able to perform their *Salah* openly.

WORDS TO KNOW:

Apologize, Devotion, Retaliate, Secure

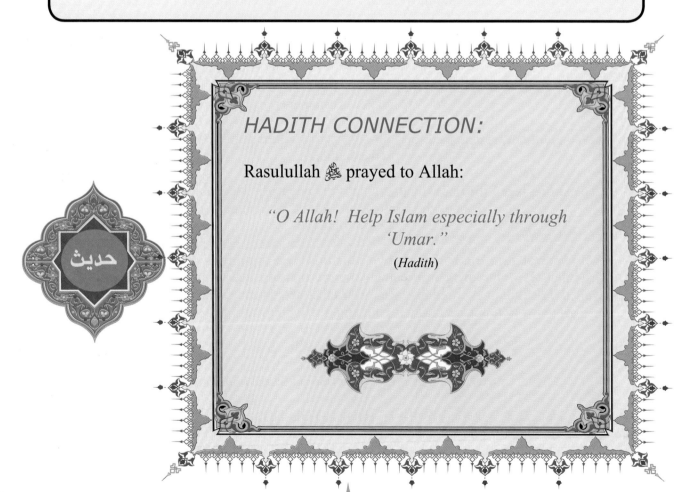

HADITH CONNECTION:

Rasulullah ﷺ prayed to Allah:

"O Allah! Help Islam especially through 'Umar."

(*Hadith*)

حديث

A Time of Test and Sorrow

The Tenth Year of the Prophethood

22 Lesson

Looking Ahead

The *Kuffar* decided it was time to punish the entire clan of Rasulullah ﷺ. Let's read about the hardships of the boycott.

The *Kuffar* tried their best to stop Rasulullah ﷺ from preaching Islam, but persecution and torture had not worked. Now they decided to boycott Rasulullah ﷺ and his entire family and clan, the Bani Hashim. A boycott is when a group of people join together in refusing to deal with a specific person or a community in order to force them to do something.

The chiefs of the *Kuffar* went to the Noble Abu Talib and said, "We've been very patient up to now, but we have waited long enough. We want you to hand Muhammad over to us so we can execute him." Abu Talib refused. "Very well then! Now you will all suffer," they said.

The *Kuffar* then forced Rasulullah ﷺ and all the members of the Bani Hashim,

A Look At History

The Quraish tribe was made up of many different clans. Some of these important clans and their members were:

Bani Hashim: Rasulullah ﷺ, 'Ali, Abu Talib, Hamza ﷺ
Bani Umayyah: 'Uthman ﷺ
Bani Ta'im: Abu Bakr ﷺ
Bani 'Adi: 'Umar ibn al-Khattab ﷺ
Bani Asad: Khadijah ﷺ, Zubair ﷺ
Bani Makhzum: Abu Jahl

Muslim and non-Muslim, to leave Makkah and stay in a barren place called the Valley of Abu Talib.

The boycott started after the *Kuffar* hung up a message on a wall of the Ka'bah. It stated that no one was to sell or give the Bani Hashim anything, no one could marry them, and no one could contact them. The Bani Hashim suffered a great deal. They often were without food and water for long periods of time. It was a very difficult time for the clan of Rasulullah ﷺ, but those who believed in the message of Islam remained patient and steadfast. Their faith in Allah ﷻ grew even stronger.

The boycott continued for almost three whole years. At last, the *Kuffar* thought Muslims had learned their lesson, and they permitted the Prophet ﷺ and the Bani Hashim to leave the valley and return to Makkah.

But the boycott caused great suffering. The conditions were so bad that they affected the health of both Abu Talib and Khadijah ﵂. Soon both of them passed away.

Abu Talib was like a father to Rasulullah ﷺ. He cared for him when he was all alone as an orphan. Later Abu Talib protected Rasulullah ﷺ from the plans the *Kuffar* had to kill him. Now with Abu Talib gone, there was no one to stand between Rasulullah ﷺ and those who wanted him dead.

Sayyidatina Khadijah ﵂ had been married to Rasulullah ﷺ for nearly 25 years. She was the mother of his children. It had been a very happy marriage. Rasulullah ﷺ was very upset with her death. He called this year the "Year of Sorrow," and he remembered his beloved wife for the rest of his life. He said, "She was my dearest companion. She helped me when my own people were my enemies."

It was the custom among Arabs before Islam to have more than one wife. But Rasulullah ﷺ was different. As long as Khadijah ﵂ was alive, he never married anyone else. His marriage to her set an example for a perfect marriage.

Years later, Rasulullah ﷺ was remarried to a lady named Sawdah ﵂, who was a widow. He also married `A'ishah ﵂, the daughter of his friend Abu Bakr ﵁. Later, Rasulullah ﷺ married other women. In all of his marriages, Rasulullah ﷺ treated his wives with justice and kindness.

WE HAVE LEARNED:

- The boycott of Rasulullah ﷺ and his family did not force the Muslims to give up Islam.
- Rasulullah ﷺ lost the two people closest to him after the boycott ended.
- His marriages show us how a man should treat his wife.

WORDS TO KNOW:

Mourned, Justice, Widow, Year of Sorrow

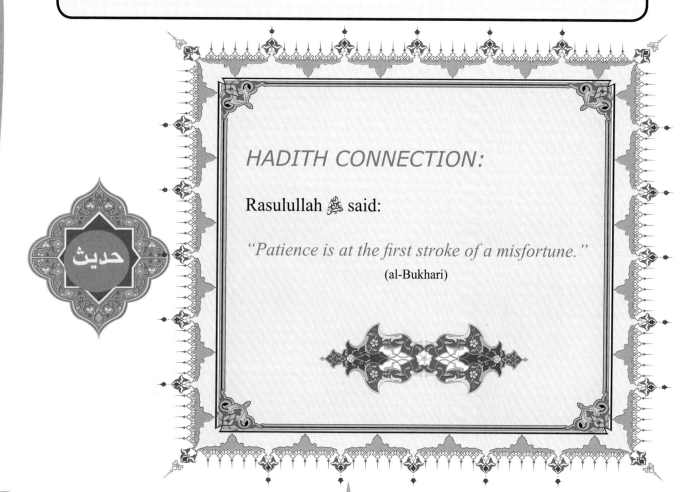

HADITH CONNECTION:

Rasulullah ﷺ said:

"Patience is at the first stroke of a misfortune."

(al-Bukhari)

Rasulullah ﷺ goes to Ta'if

23
Lesson

Looking Ahead

Rasulullah ﷺ wanted to preach Islam outside of Makkah. He went to the hill town of Ta'if. Let's read about how its people responded to the message of Islam.

In a single year, Rasulullah ﷺ had lost the loving protection of his uncle and the loving company of his wife. This made the *Kuffar* very confident that they could deal with the Prophet ﷺ. They began a new attack against Allah's Messenger ﷺ.

Rasulullah ﷺ kept on preaching the words of Allah ﷻ to the people of Makkah in spite of tremendous difficulties. One day he decided to travel to the city of Ta'if to see if the people would listen to his message. Ta'if was about 40 miles to

The rugged mountains that the Prophet ﷺ had to climb in order to reach Ta'if were difficult and dangerous.

the east of Makkah. Rasulullah ﷺ took Zaid ؓ along with him. They walked east through the desert and finally up high on the rugged mountains to reach the city.

TA'IF: A CITY IN ARABIA

The city of Ta'if was dominated by the tribe of Bani Thaqif, and it was an important religious center for the worship of the goddess al-Lat, who was called the "Lady of Ta'if." Because the city sat high up in the Sarawat Mountains, it had a milder climate than that of hot and dry Makkah. Wheat and different kinds of fruit grew there in great number. Because of this Ta'if was called the "Garden of the Hijaz." Today, over 500,000 people live in the city.

When he arrived in Ta'if, Rasulullah ﷺ began to preach to its people. "Believe in Allah!" he told them, "Beware of the Last Day!" But the people of Ta'if were even more devoted to idol-worship than the *Makkans*. This town had a huge idol of the goddess al-Lat. They were in no mood to listen to anything about *Tawhid*. They insulted Rasulullah ﷺ with bad words. They then told their children to chase him out of the town. All the children gathered stones and began to throw them at Rasulullah ﷺ. He and Zaid ؓ quickly left Ta'if.

Rasulullah ﷺ was hurt by the stones thrown by the children. He was covered with bruises and cuts, and was bleeding. As he left the city, he took shelter in a small garden. The Angel Jibril ؑ appeared and told Rasulullah ﷺ that if he so wished, he would cause the mountains to tumble down on Ta'if. Although he had been insulted and injured, Rasulullah ﷺ said no. Instead, he prayed for himself and for the people who hurt him. "O Allah, give me strength to serve you. The people of Ta'if don't know me. Forgive them and show them the path of Islam," he said.

Ten years later Allah ﷻ granted Rasulullah's prayer. The people of Ta'if, who had once driven him out with insults, accepted Islam.

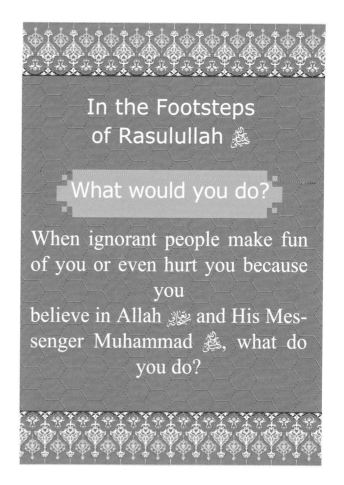

In the Footsteps of Rasulullah ﷺ

What would you do?

When ignorant people make fun of you or even hurt you because you believe in Allah ﷻ and His Messenger Muhammad ﷺ, what do you do?

WE HAVE LEARNED:

- ⟳ Rasulullah ﷺ went to Ta'if to preach Islam.
- ⟳ The people of Ta'if insulted and injured him.
- ⟳ Rasulullah ﷺ prayed to Allah ﷻ to guide the people of Ta'if.

WORDS TO KNOW:

Curse, Insult, Protection, Mild

QUR'AN CONNECTION:

Allah advised Rasulullah:

خُذِ ٱلْعَفْوَ وَأْمُرْ بِٱلْعُرْفِ
وَأَعْرِضْ عَنِ ٱلْجَٰهِلِينَ ﴿١٩٩﴾

القرآن

"O Prophet, continue to forgive; and continue to command what is right; but do not pay any attention to the ignorant."

(Surah al-A'raf 7:199)

Looking Ahead

Allah ﷻ blessed Rasulullah ﷺ with a great gift. Let's read about it in this lesson.

One night after he had returned from the trip to Ta'if, Rasulullah ﷺ was awakened from his sleep by the Angel Jibril ﷺ. "Allah is inviting you to visit the heaven," Jibril ﷺ told him. "He will show you some of His signs." It was the 27th night of the month of Rajab, one year before the *Hijrah* to Madinah.

Sayyidina Jibril ﷺ first took Rasulullah ﷺ to the Masjid al-Haram, which is the Ka'bah. There he gave him the Buraq, a heavenly creature that resembled a white horse with wings. It moved at the speed of light, which is very fast. Rasulullah ﷺ mounted the Buraq, and in an instant he was in Masjid al-Aqsa, 800 miles away in the city of Jerusalem!

Jerusalem is a special place for Muslims because of the heavenly journey of

Jerusalem: A Historical City

The city of Jerusalem is one of the oldest cities on earth. Historians believe that it has inhabited for nearly 5000 years! Around 1000 BCE the Bani Israil conquered the city and the prophet King Dawud ﷺ made Jerusalem the capital of his kingdom, and his son, King Sulaiman ﷺ, built a massive temple that became a center for the worship of the One God.

Several polytheistic empires ruled over Jerusalem. The temple built by Sulaiman was torn down. Finally in 638 CE the Muslim Arabs conquered the city from the Romans. The *Khalifah* 'Umar ﷺ had a small mosque built on the part of ruins of Prophet Sulaiman's temple.

85

Rasulullah ﷺ and the fact that several past prophets had lived there. Al-Masjid al-Aqsa, the "Furthest Mosque," had been built forty years after al-Masjid al-Haram of Makkah, according to a *Hadith* reported in Al-Bukhari.

Allah ﷻ had now miraculously caused all the previous prophets and messengers to gather in that spot to honor Prophet Muhammad ﷺ. Allah ﷻ had appointed him to lead all the prophets in *Salat*.

After he met with all of these great men, Rasullah ﷺ was taken to the heavens as he stood on a huge rock that was in the vicinity of al-Masjid al-Aqsa. Many years later, Muslims built a beautiful masjid around the rock. This masjid is called the "Masjid of the Dome of the Rock." It was a short distance from the original al-Masjid al-Aqsa.

As he journeyed through heavens, Rasulullah ﷺ met many prophets. He saw the beauty of the gardens of Paradise, which Allah ﷻ has promised to those who obey Him. He also saw the terrible sights of Hell, where sinful people will go after death.

Prophet Muhammad ﷺ soared to the highest Heaven with Angel Jirbril عليه السلام. He reached a place called *Sidrat ul-Muntaha*. There the two stopped. Angel Jibril عليه السلام said, "I can go no further. From here you must go alone." No angel or human being had ever been past *Sidrat ul-Muntaha* before, and no one else would ever go there.

But Rasulullah went forward. Allah raised Prophet Muhammad ﷺ higher than any other of His creations by bringing him so near to Him. How much Allah ﷻ loves and has blessed Muhammad, His last prophet!

Allah ﷻ spoke directly to Rasulullah ﷺ and made five daily prayers a duty for Muslims. When we make *sajda* before Allah in *Salah* we are very close to Him. Rasulullah ﷺ once said, "*Salah* is the Mi'raj of a believer."

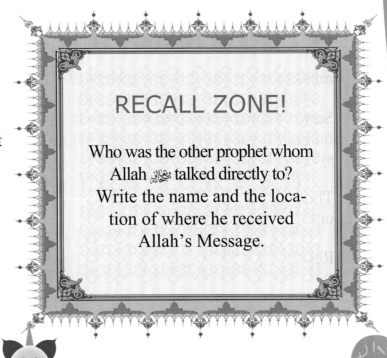

RECALL ZONE!

Who was the other prophet whom Allah ﷻ talked directly to? Write the name and the location of where he received Allah's Message.

Allah ﷻ then told Rasulullah ﷺ to return to Earth. When he returned to his bed he found that it was still warm! How could Mi'raj have taken place? It was a miracle! But Allah ﷻ has power over everything and can do whatever He wills.

The next day, Rasulullah ﷺ told people about his night journey. The *kuffar*, of course, mocked him. But his dear friend Abu Bakr ﷺ said, "Muhammad always speaks the truth. If angels can come to him from heaven every day, then he can also visit heaven. Allah ﷻ has power over everything!"

The Speed of Light:

What does it mean when the Buraq traveled almost as fast as The Speed of Light?

Einstein's Theory of Relativity says that nothing in the universe can travel faster than the velocity (the rate at which an object changes position) of light.

Light is part of the electromagnetic spectrum, which includes radio waves, micro-waves, infrared radiation, visible light, ultraviolet radiation, X-rays and gamma rays.

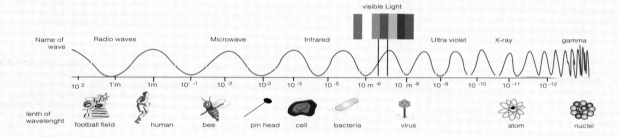

In a vacuum (the absence of matter), the speed of light is always 299,792,458 meters per second.

But light does change its speed when it moves from one object to another. So for light to travel from the Moon to the Earth, it takes about 1.2 seconds and it takes about 8 minutes from the Sun's light to hit the Earth.

Suppose you flip on a light, you might think there's no delay between when we see the bulb glowing and the light reaching the corners of the room. However, our nervous system is too slow to notice the rays of light appearing from the bulb.

Think of other examples in which you can measure the speed of light traveling from one object to another.

Resources: http://encyclopedia.kids.net.au, http://science.hq.nasa.gov and http://unmuseum.mus.pa.us

WE HAVE LEARNED:

- Rasulullah ﷺ rode on the Buraq from the Ka'bah (Masjid al-Haram) to Masjid al-Aqsa in Jerusalem. This is called Isra'.
- Rasulullah ﷺ ascended from the rock to heaven, which is called Mi'raj.
- Allah commanded Muslims to pray five times each day.

WORDS TO KNOW:

Masjid al-Aqsa, Masjid al-Haram, Mi'raj, Appoint, Buraq, Dome of the Rock, Prostrate, Signs of Allah

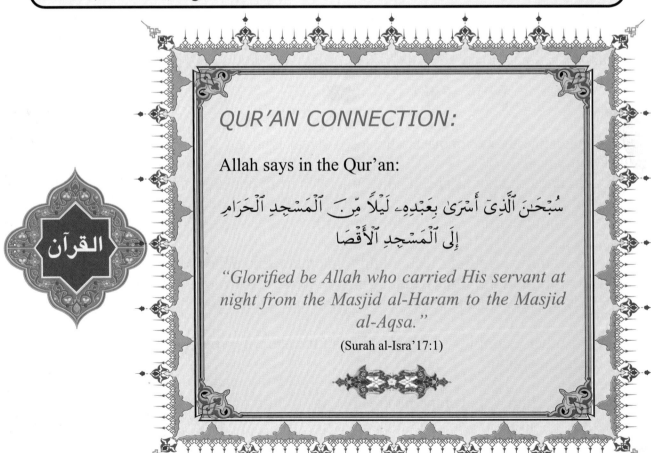

القرآن

QUR'AN CONNECTION:

Allah says in the Qur'an:

سُبْحَٰنَ ٱلَّذِىٓ أَسْرَىٰ بِعَبْدِهِۦ لَيْلًا مِّنَ ٱلْمَسْجِدِ ٱلْحَرَامِ إِلَى ٱلْمَسْجِدِ ٱلْأَقْصَا

"Glorified be Allah who carried His servant at night from the Masjid al-Haram to the Masjid al-Aqsa."

(Surah al-Isra' 17:1)

Rasulullah ﷺ Talks to the People of Yathrib

25 Lesson

Looking Ahead

Islam began to spread outside of Makkah. Many people in Yathrib accepted Islam. They invited Rasulullah ﷺ and the Muslims to come to live in their city. Let's read about what happened next.

Once a year, people from all over Arabia would come to Makkah to make the pilgrimage. This was a practice from the days of Prophet Ibrahim ﷺ, although people had long forgotten the true meaning of it. Instead of worshipping the One God, they now came to Makkah to pray to their idols.

MADINAH AL-MUNAWWARAH

In pre-Islamic times Madinah was known as Yathrib. Compared to Makkah, a busy and sophisticated trading town, Yathrib was an agricultural settlement. It was situated in a mountain basin on the western edge of the plateau of Western Arabia, some 90 miles from the shores of the Red Sea. The town had plentiful water resources and lands made fertile by ancient lava flows.

The land was full with citrus groves, grapes, figs, wheat, almonds and dates. These rich agricultural crops provided plenty of livelihoods for the people who lived in Yathrib.

Yathrib was inhabited by the pagan Arab tribes and some Jewish tribes at the time of the birth of Muhammad ﷺ. The two powerful tribes of Banu Aws and Banu Khazraj were involved in fierce battles with each other for a long time. In 618 a great war broke out involving almost all the clans of Yathrib and it resulted in heavy death tolls. The people of Yathrib were so tired of the fighting that when they heard of the noble work and message of Muhammad ﷺ, they sent some of their envoys to Makkah to talk to the Prophet ﷺ and ask for his help in settling the dispute.

With the order from Allah ﷻ, the Prophet ﷺ accepted the offer and asked the Muslims to move to Yathrib. He left for Madinah with his friend Abu Bakr ﷺ when all the Muslims reached to Madinah safely. Ali ﷺ joined him on the way.

The migration of the Prophet ﷺ from Makkah to Yathrib is known as *Hijra* and marks the beginning of Islamic calendar. It was July, 16, 622 of the Gregarian calendar.

89

Nearly 11 years after he received the first *Wahi*, Rasulullah ﷺ met six people from the city of Yathrib during their pilgrimage to Makkah. He used the time to talk to them about Islam. The men from Yathrib knew that the Jewish tribes of their city often spoke of a great prophet who would come soon and they realized that Muhammad ﷺ must be that prophet. They were so glad to have met Rasulullah ﷺ that they quickly accepted Islam.

When the men returned to Madinah, they told others about their visit with the Prophet ﷺ. They talked about the noble and wonderful qualities they saw in him. Many people in Madinah were ready to travel the 250 miles to Makkah in order to meet Rasulullah ﷺ themselves.

The following year many more people came to Makkah to meet with the Prophet ﷺ. All of them accepted Islam. The people of Yathrib also invited Rasulullah ﷺ and the Muslims to migrate to their city. They made a pledge to Rasulullah ﷺ. "We shall protect you as we protect our families against all our enemies," they promised.

Rasulullah ﷺ was very pleased to hear this. He also made a pledge to the people of Madinah. "My blood is your blood," he said. "I am one of you. You are of me. I shall never leave you. In peace and in war, I'll live with you until I die."

Rasulullah ﷺ called the people of Madinah Ansar, or the helpers. The people of Madinah were the "helpers" of Allah, of Rasulullah ﷺ and of Islam.

The *Kuffar* were very angry when they learned about this. They became even crueler to the Muslims, and Allah ﷻ asked His prophet to send the Muslims out of Makkah to Madinah.

Rasulullah ﷺ told the Muslims about Allah's command. Of course, it was hard for the Muslims to leave their families, friends, and homes, but they were always ready to do what Allah ﷻ and His prophet wanted them to do. Soon almost all the Muslims had left for Madinah.

RECALL ZONE!

Talk to your friend about the 'first *Hijrah*' of the Muslims.

Do you remember the country they migrated to?

This was the second *Hijrah* for many of the Muslims. Freedom to practice Islam is very important to Muslims. It is more important than one's house, property, friends, relatives, and country. One who makes *Hijrah* is called a *Muhajir*. Allah ﷻ has promised a great reward for those who make *Hijrah* for His cause.

WE HAVE LEARNED:

- Many people of Madinah (Yathrib) accepted Islam.
- These Muslims invited Rasulullah ﷺ and the Muslims to come to live in their city.
- The Muslims were asked by Allah ﷻ to make *Hijrah* to Madinah.

WORDS TO KNOW:

Muhajir, Hijra, Afterlife, Harsh, Popular

QUR'AN CONNECTION:

القرآن

Allah says in the Qur'an:

وَٱلسَّٰبِقُونَ ٱلْأَوَّلُونَ مِنَ ٱلْمُهَٰجِرِينَ وَٱلْأَنصَارِ وَٱلَّذِينَ ٱتَّبَعُوهُم بِإِحْسَٰنٍ رَّضِىَ ٱللَّهُ عَنْهُمْ وَرَضُواْ عَنْهُ وَأَعَدَّ لَهُمْ جَنَّٰتٍ تَجْرِى تَحْتَهَا ٱلْأَنْهَٰرُ خَٰلِدِينَ فِيهَآ أَبَدًا ذَٰلِكَ ٱلْفَوْزُ ٱلْعَظِيمُ ۝

"The very first, among the Muhajirun and Ansar and those who follow them with good deeds, Allah is well pleased with them, and they are pleased with Him. And Allah has made Paradise ready for them under which rivers flow, to live there forever.

This is the greatest success."

(Surah at-Tawbah 9:100)

Rasulullah ﷺ makes Hijrah to Madinah

Looking Ahead

The *Kuffar* decided to finish off Rasulullah ﷺ once and for all. Allah ﷻ asked him to leave for Yathrib. Let's read about it in this lesson.

When the Makkan *Kuffar* learned about the success of Islam in Madinah, they became very worried. They didn't want Rasulullah ﷺ or the Muslims to go to Madinah. They were afraid that one day the Muslims might become very powerful.

The leaders of the *Kuffar* met to discuss this problem. They decided that they had to kill Rasulullah ﷺ. "If Muhammad were dead," they thought, "we could deal with the Muslims in both Makkah and Madinah."

Allah informed Rasulullah ﷺ about the plans of the *Kuffar*. He told him to make *Hijrah* to Madinah and live there with the Muslims.

Rasulullah ﷺ made plans to leave and discussed them with his friend Abu Bakr ﷺ.

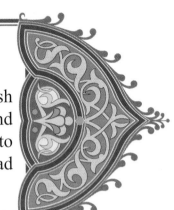

RECALL ZONE!

How did Allah ﷻ communicate with Rasulullah ﷺ?

Think about it and write a paragraph with your explanation on a separate piece of paper

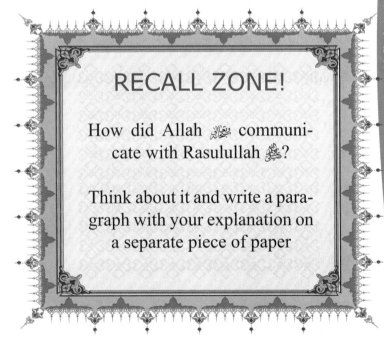

Abu Bakr ﷺ got ready to go with Rasulullah ﷺ.

One night the *Kuffar* decided to kill Rasulullah ﷺ. They went to his house and waited silently for him to come out.

That same night, Allah ﷻ asked His prophet to leave for Madinah.

Rasulullah ﷺ was ready. But one thing troubled him. Since everyone trusted him, many Makkan *Kuffar* had given him their money and other valuable things for safe-keeping. He wanted to return these things to their owners. Although Rasulullah's life was in danger, he couldn't forget the trust of the people.

He asked his cousin 'Ali ؓ to stay behind and return those things to their owners the next morning. 'Ali ؓ gladly agreed. When the Prophet ﷺ left, 'Ali ؓ went to sleep in the Prophet's bed. He was a brave man and a true Muslim. He wasn't afraid that the *Kuffar* might mistake him for Rasulullah ﷺ and kill him.

Rasulullah ﷺ left his house. As he walked past the *Kuffar* he recited verses from the Qur'an. At that moment Allah ﷻ blinded the unbelievers so they couldn't see him.

Rasulullah ﷺ and Abu Bakr ؓ left Makkah that night. They knew that they could not take the main road to Yathrib because the *Kuffar* would look there first. So they decided to go south, which was in the opposite direction, wait for a few days, and then travel north to Yathrib.

In the early morning, they hid in a mountain a few miles south of Makkah called Thawr. They climbed the mountain to spend the day hiding from the *Kuffar* and wait for Abu Bakr's servant to come with camels.

Later that day the *Kuffar* found out that Rasulullah ﷺ had left. They sent out men in all directions hoping to capture the Prophet ﷺ. A small group of them headed south. They came to the foot of Mount Thawr and spotted a cave high up on the mountain. The *Kuffar* decided that it would be best to check the cave in case the Prophet ﷺ was hiding in it. They quickly climbed the mountain.

Sitting at the entrance of the cave Prophet ﷺ and Abu Bakr ؓ could see the *Kuffar* climbing towards them. Abu Bakr ؓ became worried; but not worried for himself. He was troubled what might happen to Rasulullah ﷺ if he were to be captured. But the Prophet told him not to worry. Allah ﷻ would protect them. Then, by a miracle, a dove flew to the opening of the cave and laid her eggs in a nest at the cave's entrance. A spider also quickly wove its web across the entrance. After a several minutes climb, the *Kuffar* reached the cave. But when they saw the bird's eggs and the spider's web, they thought, "No one has gone in here recently. Let's go." And they went away without looking inside the cave at all.

Prophet Muhammad ﷺ and Abu Bakr ﷺ hid in the cave for three days. They waited for things to quiet down. Then their camels came and they left quietly for Madinah.

A photograph of the Cave of Thawr where the Prophet ﷺ and Abu Bakr ﷺ hid from the *Kuffar*.

WE HAVE LEARNED:

- When the *Kuffar* decided to kill Rasulullah ﷺ, Allah ﷻ asked him to leave for Madinah.
- Rasulullah ﷺ asked 'Ali ؓ to return people's money and valuables to them.
- Allah ﷻ made the *Kuffar* blind, and Prophet Muhammad ﷺ left with his friend, Abu Bakr ؓ, in the night.

WORDS TO KNOW:

Thawr, Success, Trust, Valuables

HADITH CONNECTION:

Leaving Makkah, Rasulullah ﷺ prayed to Allah ﷻ:

"O Allah, you know well that my enemies have expelled me from this city of Makkah, which is very dear to me. Now take me to live in the city which is dear to You."

(Hadith)

حديث

Love for Rasulullah

Looking Ahead

It is absolutely imperative for Muslims to have love for the Prophet Muhammad ﷺ. Let's read about why in this lesson.

The love of Prophet Muhammad ﷺ is a gift Allah ﷻ gave to the believers. No prophet has loved his *Ummah* as much as the Prophet ﷺ loved his *Ummah*. No *Ummah* before ever loved and obeyed their prophet as much as the *Ummah* of Muhammad ﷺ loves him. Love of Rasullullah ﷺ is based upon many factors: It is part of our love of Allah and it is also a commitment to follow Rasullullah ﷺ. Allah ﷻ says in the Qur'an:

قُلْ إِن كُنتُمْ تُحِبُّونَ ٱللَّهَ فَٱتَّبِعُونِي يُحْبِبْكُمُ ٱللَّهُ وَيَغْفِرْ لَكُمْ ذُنُوبَكُمْ ۚ وَٱللَّهُ غَفُورٌ رَّحِيمٌ ۝

"Say (O Muhammad), if you love Allah then follow me, then Allah will love you and forgive you your sins: for Allah is most forgiving and most merciful."
(Surah Al 'Imran 3:31)

We worship Allah ﷻ by following the *Sunnah* of Rasulullah ﷺ. It is through his teachings that we came to know the truth about One God and our duties to Him. Rasulullah's mission was to lead us to proper belief. By following his *Sunnah* we become worthy of Allah's love, forgiveness, and mercy.

The revelation of the Qur'an is from Allah ﷻ. He Himself safeguards it. Rasulullah conveyed the message to humanity as he received it from Angel Jibril ﷺ. The Qur'an confirms it:

وَمَا يَنطِقُ عَنِ ٱلْهَوَىٰ ۝ إِنْ هُوَ إِلَّا وَحْيٌ يُوحَىٰ ۝ عَلَّمَهُ شَدِيدُ ٱلْقُوَىٰ ۝

"He (Muhammad) does not speak of his desire. It is a Wahi, revealed to him. He is taught by One mighty in power."
(Surah An-Najm 53:3-5)

Rasulullah ﷺ was given the knowledge by Allah ﷻ to explain the teachings of the Qur'an. He was also sent as a true role model to be followed:

لَّقَدْ كَانَ لَكُمْ فِى رَسُولِ ٱللَّهِ أُسْوَةٌ حَسَنَةٌ لِّمَن كَانَ يَرْجُواْ ٱللَّهَ وَٱلْيَوْمَ ٱلْأَخِرَ وَذَكَرَ ٱللَّهَ كَثِيرًا ۝

"You have indeed in the Messenger of Allah an excellent example for those who have hope in Allah and the final Day, and who remember Allah much."
(Surah Al-Ahzab 33:21)

The character of Rasulullah ﷺ is a true and everlasting model of ideal behavior for all humankind. Obeying and loving him brings the blessings of this world and of the Hereafter. Therefore Allah ﷻ enjoins upon us:

مَّن يُطِعِ ٱلرَّسُولَ فَقَدْ أَطَاعَ ٱللَّهَ

"He who obeys the messenger, obeys Allah..."
(Surah An-Nisa' 4:80)

Rasulullah ﷺ was sent as a mercy for all of humanity and all the worlds, not just those who follow him. His heart was always distressed for all people who were misguided by the Shaitan. However, for the believers he was even more concerned:

لَقَدْ جَآءَكُمْ رَسُولٌ مِّنْ أَنفُسِكُمْ عَزِيزٌ عَلَيْهِ مَا عَنِتُّمْ حَرِيصٌ عَلَيْكُم بِٱلْمُؤْمِنِينَ رَءُوفٌ رَّحِيمٌ ۝

"Now has come to you a messenger from among you; it grieves him that you
should suffer, ardently anxious is he for you, to the believers he is most kind."
(Surah At-Tawbah 9:128)

Rasulullah was concerned for the well-being of humankind, and therefore we love him from the depth of our hearts. Rasulullah ﷺ loves all those who believe, even more than we love ourselves. Allah ﷻ tells us:

ٱلنَّبِىُّ أَوْلَىٰ بِٱلْمُؤْمِنِينَ مِنْ أَنفُسِهِمْ وَأَزْوَٰجُهُ أُمَّهَٰتُهُمْ

"The Prophet is closer to the believers than their own selves, and his wives are their mothers."
(Surah Al-Ahzab 33:6)

Since Allah ﷻ asks us to follow Rasulullah ﷺ, He also made sure to safeguard the *Sunnah* for us. No other human being before modern times has left such a detailed record of his life and teachings as did our Prophet ﷺ. And no people in history have preserved the teachings of their supreme religious leader so well as did the Muslims.

Our love of the Prophet ﷺ is a commandment from Allah ﷻ, and our own thankfulness to Rasulullah ﷺ comes from his love for us. These are beautiful emotions that reside in our hearts. However it is much more than a way of life that we practice. He has left a legacy that lives in us, members of his *Ummah*.

WE HAVE LEARNED:

- ✑ The love for Prophet Muhammad ﷺ is a gift from Allah ﷻ to the believers.
- ✑ Rasulullah ﷺ was sent as a mercy not only for the believers but for all humanity.
- ✑ Our love of the Prophet ﷺ is a commandment from Allah ﷻ.

WORDS TO KNOW:

Ideal, Everlasting, Legacy

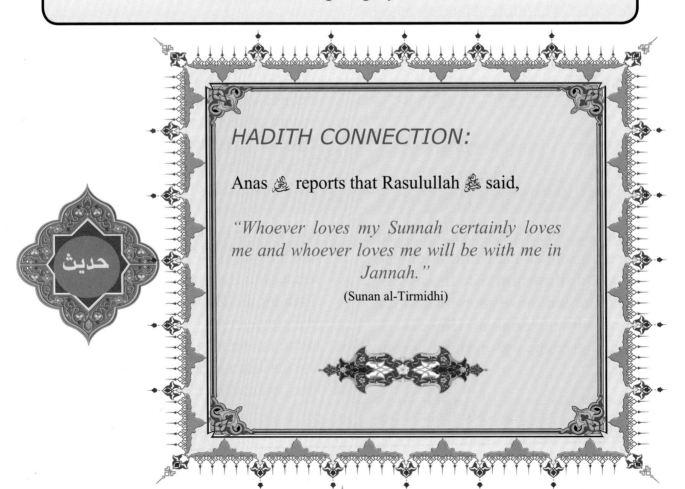

HADITH CONNECTION:

Anas ﷜ reports that Rasulullah ﷺ said,

"Whoever loves my Sunnah certainly loves me and whoever loves me will be with me in Jannah."

(Sunan al-Tirmidhi)

حديث

The Life of Rasulullah ﷺ before Prophethood

28 Lesson

Looking Ahead

Rasulullah ﷺ was a special individual even before he received *Wahi*. Let's find out why.

In this book we studied the life of Rasulullah ﷺ while he lived in Makkah. For forty years he led his life as an extraordinary person. He refused to take part in the corrupt culture that surrounded him. When people worshipped many gods, he looked for One God. At a time when people thought it was normal to cheat and tell falsehoods, he always told the truth.

In his fortieth year Muhammad ﷺ received the first revelations of the Qur'an, which changed his life completely. Without his prophethood our world would have been very different place. So let us review his life before the mission of Prophethood.

Rasulullah ﷺ was a very extraordinary individual. We read about the miracles that occurred at his birth as well as the sadness he faced as an orphan. He was a lov-

RECALL ZONE!

Do you remember the name of the war and the names of the fighting tribes, which ended only after the treaty of al-Fudul?

Why did Rasulullah ﷺ always remember the Hilf al-Fudul?

ing child who brought many blessings to the household of Halimah ﷺ, his foster-mother. As teenager he was known for his honesty and trustworthiness. These characteristics became, in fact, his nicknames, *as-Sadiq* and *al-Amin*. He did not like tribal feuds and fights, but rather he preferred peace, like the Hilf al-Fudul.

Young Muhammad ﷺ always tried to be a peacemaker. He found a beautiful way to help Makkan clans share the honor of placing the Hajr al-Aswad back into its place. He was an honest businessman and his trade made profits. It was his honesty that endeared him to Khadijah ﷺ, which led to their marriage.

This was his beautiful character before the *Wahi*. Muhammad ﷺ earned everyone's respect because of these qualities. These very same qualities also made him a successful businessman and husband to a wonderful woman named Khadijah ﷺ.

Nevertheless he did not have the qualities that would have made him a leader of the *Makkans*. Before Islam, the Arabs admired their leaders for their wealth and arrogance, and at times, violent behavior. Muhammad ﷺ had none of these negative traits. Bravery and pride in one's tribe was very important for leadership. In fact much of Arabic poetry before Islam deals with wars and tales of heroism.

The Arabs greatly admired poets, and they were seen as celebrities in their society. Yet most of their poetry had no moral lessons encouraging people to do good deeds. Most of it was about heroic battles of the past; they created great pride in war. These also ignited the flames of reprisal and revenge.

Rasulullah lived, in fact, in a very rough society. His people drank alcohol in great quantities, gambled away their money in games of chance, and cheated their customers in business. The Arab clans and tribes were feuding and fighting each other, much like gangs do today. People were proud of their clans and tribes. They regarded themselves as being superior to all the other tribes, even though they were all Arabs. Muhammad's own tribe, the Quraish, was so proud of itself that they regarded all tribes as being below their honor.

Non-Arab outsiders (like Ethiopians or Persians) had no place in this tribal society. Women had few rights, and they were treated like the property of their husbands. Many times a father would bury alive his baby daughter out of embarrassment for not having had a son. Slaves, orphans, widows, and the poor were treated very badly.

Muhammad ﷺ thought about the bad condition of his people, but had no solution. He began to look for a higher power.

WE HAVE LEARNED:

- ⌛ Rasulullah ﷺ was a very unusual person from the time of his birth.
- ⌛ Rasulullah ﷺ never worshipped idols like the other Arabs did.
- ⌛ All of Makkah had great respect for him.

WORDS TO KNOW:

Pre-Islamic, Celebrity, Poet, Reprisal

القرآن

QUR'AN CONNECTION:

Allah tells us that no matter how beautiful its words are, the Qur'an is not poetry:

وَمَا عَلَّمْنَٰهُ ٱلشِّعْرَ وَمَا يَنۢبَغِى لَهُۥٓ إِنْ هُوَ إِلَّا ذِكْرٌ وَقُرْءَانٌ مُّبِينٌ ﴿٦٩﴾

"And We have not taught him (Muhammad) poetry, nor is it appropriate for him. This is nothing else than a reminder and a lecture making plain…"

(Surah Ya Sin 36:69)

The Life of Rasulullah ﷺ after Prophethood

Looking Ahead

Receiving *Wahi* from Allah ﷻ changed not only Rasulullah ﷺ but the course of history. Let's read about how this happened.

In past lessons we have come to understand that Rasulullah ﷺ did not possess any of the characteristics of leadership that most Arabs admired. He did not approve of the ways the people of his days led their lives.

Disappointed as he was with the culture of his Arab people, Muhammad ﷺ could find no way to encourage people behave for the better. Therefore he decided to withdraw from the world. He made regular trips to the cave Hira to meditate and look for his Creator. There one day he received *Wahi*, the revelation: "Read in the name of your Lord who created."

This *Wahi* would continue for 13 years in Makkah and ten years in Madinah. It was a revelation that would bring to completion of all previous revelations. It was the same message that was revealed to Ibrahim, Musa, Dawud and 'Isa ﷺ.

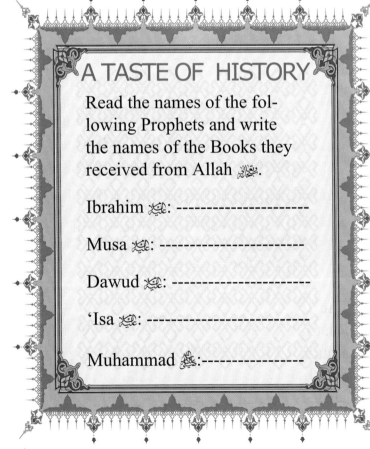

A TASTE OF HISTORY

Read the names of the following Prophets and write the names of the Books they received from Allah ﷻ.

Ibrahim ﷺ: ----------------------

Musa ﷺ: -------------------------

Dawud ﷺ: ----------------------

'Isa ﷺ: ---------------------------

Muhammad ﷺ:-------------------

The *Wahi* of the Qur'an would be safe-guarded by Allah ﷻ forever. There would not be any change in the message, and there would be no need of another prophet, messenger, or book after it. The knowledge Rasulullah ﷺ received was directly from Allah ﷻ through His trusted angel, Jibril ﷺ. Rasulullah ﷺ himself said:

أَدَّبَنِي رَبِّي فَأَحْسَنَ تَأْدِيبِي.

"My Lord taught me and that is the best knowledge."

In this way an orphan who never went to school became the greatest teacher of humankind by the command of Allah ﷻ. This divine knowledge is the greatest miracle of Rasulullah ﷺ. The Qur'an also tells us the role of Rasulullah ﷺ as the teacher:

كَمَآ أَرْسَلْنَا فِيكُمْ رَسُولًا مِّنكُمْ يَتْلُواْ عَلَيْكُمْ ءَايَـٰتِنَا وَيُزَكِّيكُمْ وَيُعَلِّمُكُمُ ٱلْكِتَـٰبَ وَٱلْحِكْمَةَ وَيُعَلِّمُكُم مَّا لَمْ تَكُونُواْ تَعْلَمُونَ ﴿١٥١﴾

"As We have sent among you a Messenger of your own, reciting to you our verses, and purifying you, and instructing you in the Book and Wisdom, and teaching you new knowledge that you knew not."

(Surah Al-Baqarah 2:151)

The first thing this verse says is that Rasulullah ﷺ was one of us, meaning a human being. Yet he is a human like no other. He was chosen by Allah ﷻ to carry out a very special task. His wisdom would teach us how to be good servants of Allah ﷻ and worthy of His love. As a

human being he taught us how to practice the message of the Qur'an. He was, as the Mother of the Believers, A'ishah, said: "His manners were the Qur'an."

He practiced what the Qur'an taught. He was our true role model. If he were not human he could have never been a true model. As a human being he had passed through all the human experiences. In each case he set the best example for us.

Rasulullah ﷺ also taught us *Tazkiyah*: inner and outer purification. The outer purification of our bodies, clothes, and environment is also described as *Taharah*. However, bodily purification (*Taharah*) is not enough for a life of faith. We need purification of our souls as well. This is called *Tazkiyat an-Nafs*. Allah ﷻ has given our souls two choices:

وَنَفْسٍ وَمَا سَوَّىٰهَا ﴿٧﴾ فَأَلْهَمَهَا فُجُورَهَا وَتَقْوَىٰهَا ﴿٨﴾ قَدْ أَفْلَحَ مَن زَكَّىٰهَا ﴿٩﴾ وَقَدْ خَابَ مَن دَسَّىٰهَا ﴿١٠﴾

"By the soul and the share and command given to it, and its inspiration as to what is wrong and what is right, truly he succeeds who purifies it, and he fails who corrupts it."

(Surah Ash-Shams 91:7-10)

Rasulullah ﷺ taught us *Tazkiyah* to help us choose between right and wrong. All of our praying, fasting, *Zakah*, and going on *Hajj* have no meaning if we offer them without sincerity.

The third task of Rasulullah ﷺ was to teach Allah's book, the Qur'an. Rasulullah ﷺ gained knowledge of the meanings of the *Ayats* from the Angel Jibril ﷺ and then he taught them to his *Sahabah*. The *Sahabah* taught this knowledge to the Tabi'un, the generation that came after. This teaching continues even to our times. In this way Allah ﷻ safeguards the Qur'an and protects its teachings.

Allah ﷻ blessed Rasulullah ﷺ with *Hikmah*, wisdom. Rasulullah's *Hikmah* was inspired by Allah ﷻ. This *Hikmah* is called *Sunnah*, and it is saved in the books of *Hadith*. The *Hikmah* makes clear the meanings of the Qur'an and further explains it in a simple and beautiful way. The *Hikmah* completes the teachings of the Qur'an. Thus the Qur'an and *Sunnah* are two most genuine sources of Islamic *Shari'ah,* Islamic Law.

Allah ﷻ gave Rasulullah ﷺ knowledge of things that we do not know. Human beings gain most of their knowledge through their five senses (sight, touch, taste, smell, and hearing). Some things we discover through scholarly research and scientific experiments. We should look for wisdom everywhere. Rasulullah ﷺ said:

"Hikmah is the lost property of a believer; he takes it wherever he finds it."

(Tirmidhi, Ibn Majah)

The Qur'an also enjoins us to look at Allah's creations and reflect and think about them. However, there are many things that we cannot experience through the five senses. There are many mysteries that we can know about only through revelation. It is through revelation that we know about Allah ﷻ, the angels, the purpose of human beings, and *al-Akhirah*.

Rasulullah ﷺ is the most perfect teacher we have and all the knowledge he brought is important for us. It will always be important to all human beings.

WE HAVE LEARNED:

- Even though Rasulullah ﷺ did not learn how to read and write, he became the greatest teacher of all time.
- Allah ﷻ gave Rasulullah ﷺ knowledge of things that we do not know.
- Allah ﷻ safeguards the Qur'an and protects its teachings.

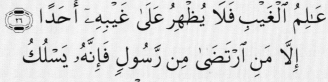

WORDS TO KNOW:

Divine, Genuine, *Hikmah*, *Tazkiyah*

القرآن

QUR'AN CONNECTION:

Allah knows everything seen and unseen. He has given information of things we don't know to His messengers:

عَٰلِمُ ٱلْغَيْبِ فَلَا يُظْهِرُ عَلَىٰ غَيْبِهِۦٓ أَحَدًا ﴿٢٦﴾ إِلَّا مَنِ ٱرْتَضَىٰ مِن رَّسُولٍ فَإِنَّهُۥ يَسْلُكُ مِنۢ بَيْنِ يَدَيْهِ وَمِنْ خَلْفِهِۦ رَصَدًا ﴿٢٧﴾

"(Allah) is the Knower of the Unseen and He reveals unto none His secret, except unto every Messenger whom He has chosen..."

(Surah al-Jinn 72:26-27)

105

Teaching the Qur'an in Makkah

Lesson 30

Looking Ahead

The most important lesson which Rasulullah ﷺ taught to all of us was the belief in *Tawhid*. He taught us to say and believe in *Shahadah*:

The world had seen many wise leaders, philosophers, spiritual teachers, military commanders, and social reformers. Among the wise men of the world, the prophets of Allah ﷻ are the noblest and highest people for us to follow. These individuals did not speak from their thoughts but through the Wisdom of Allah ﷻ that they received through revelation.

For this reason the teachings of the prophets were often opposed to the customs of the community. Instead of being popular with people, they become hated and opposed, especially by the leaders of society. Sometimes these prophets were even tortured and expelled from their homes.

However, the prophets were always steadfast in their cause. Their teachings did not change because of social pressure, worldly temptation or force. Ultimately

they succeeded, and society changed according to their teachings. The life and teachings of Rasulullah ﷺ are clear examples of this. Since he is the last of all the prophets, his teachings are complete and his life is complete. His life offers us the best examples for our life.

The *Makkans* knew the pure character of Muhammad ﷺ before he became the Messenger of Allah. It was expected that when the revelation of Allah ﷻ came they would trust him and believe his words. Unfortunately, only few righteous people accepted Rasulullah ﷺ and followed him. The majority opposed Rasulullah ﷺ, since Islam demanded that they change their old customs and ways of thinking.

One of the reasons why the *Makkans* opposed Islam was because of *Tawhid*.

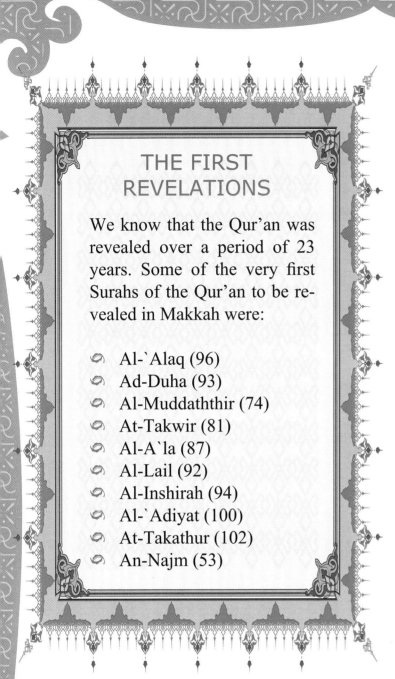

THE FIRST REVELATIONS

We know that the Qur'an was revealed over a period of 23 years. Some of the very first Surahs of the Qur'an to be revealed in Makkah were:

- Al-`Alaq (96)
- Ad-Duha (93)
- Al-Muddaththir (74)
- At-Takwir (81)
- Al-A`la (87)
- Al-Lail (92)
- Al-Inshirah (94)
- Al-`Adiyat (100)
- At-Takathur (102)
- An-Najm (53)

To accept Allah ﷻ as the only God meant giving up the many gods and goddesses they worshipped since childhood. Their ancestors forgot the One God, the *Rabb ul-`Alamin*, the "Lord of the Worlds," whom Ibrahim ﷺ spoke of. The Arabs could not understand that lifeless idols made of wood and stone could not even help themselves, much less help their worshippers.

Acceptance of the Qur'an also meant accepting that all people are the children of

Adam ﷺ and Hawwa ﷺ. Differences in race, color, language and culture are only signs of Allah's endless creative power. There is no preference of one people over another in these external characteristics. The concept of human equality is at the center of *Tawhid*.

The *Makkans* found it hard to accept that they could be equal to slaves and servants, for the message of equality also meant that women, slaves, and orphans were entitled to be respected as God's creation.

Another aspect of *Tawhid* is the belief in the *Akhirah*, the Hereafter. Whatever we do in this life is taken into account on the Day of Judgment. In the *Akhirah* we will be judged for our beliefs and actions. Most Arabs before Islam did not believe in the *Akhirah*, much less being held accountable for their actions before God! That is why the *Ayats* that were revealed in Makkah deal mostly with the Day of Judgment and the *Akhirah*, a period of existence when all of us will be raised from the dead to face judgment.

In Makkah the Muslims had to go through many tests and trials. The Qur'an advised them to use patience, rely on Allah's help and to be steadfast in their faith.

Allah ﷻ did not allow the Muslims in Makkah to retaliate, even when the *Kuffar* tortured and killed them. Their *Jihad* was not a fight against the injustice caused to them, but a striving for inner purification. Allah ﷻ strengthened their faith with the trials of suffering. The patience of the believers in this adversity actually attracted many people to Islam. The Qur'an says about these early followers:

وَٱلسَّٰبِقُونَ ٱلْأَوَّلُونَ مِنَ ٱلْمُهَٰجِرِينَ وَٱلْأَنصَارِ وَٱلَّذِينَ ٱتَّبَعُوهُم بِإِحْسَٰنٍ رَّضِىَ ٱللَّهُ عَنْهُمْ وَرَضُواْ عَنْهُ وَأَعَدَّ لَهُمْ جَنَّٰتٍ تَجْرِى تَحْتَهَا ٱلْأَنْهَٰرُ خَٰلِدِينَ فِيهَآ أَبَدًا ذَٰلِكَ ٱلْفَوْزُ ٱلْعَظِيمُ ۝

"And the first ones who led the way to Islam, the Muhajirun and Ansar, and those who follow them in their good deeds, Allah is pleased with them and they are well pleased with Him…"

(Surah At-Tawbah (9:100))

May Allah ﷻ include us among "those who follow them in their good deeds." And may Allah ﷻ send His endless blessings on our master, the Crown of Creation, the Prophet Muhammad ﷺ, and may peace be upon his holy family and righteous companions. *Amin!*

WE HAVE LEARNED:

- ☜ The Makkans knew the pure character of Muhammad ﷺ before he became a messenger of Allah ﷻ.
- ☜ The life and teachings of Rasulullah ﷺ are clear examples of his steadfastness.
- ☜ Allah ﷻ strengthened the faith of the early Muslims with trials of suffering.

WORDS TO KNOW:

Retaliate, *Tawhid*, Entitle, *Akhirah*

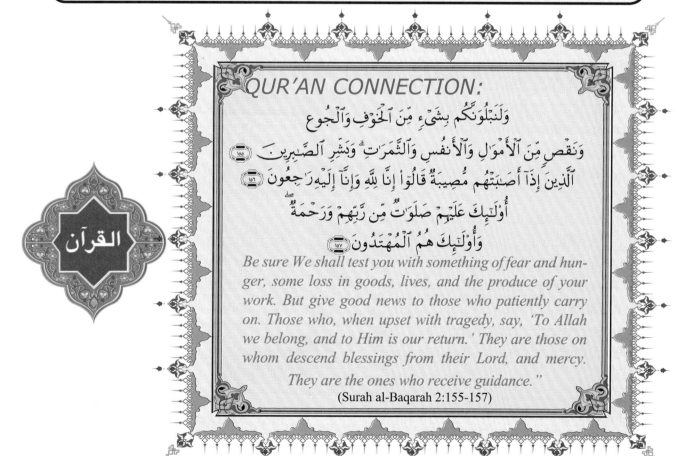

QUR'AN CONNECTION:

وَلَنَبْلُوَنَّكُم بِشَىْءٍ مِّنَ ٱلْخَوْفِ وَٱلْجُوعِ
وَنَقْصٍ مِّنَ ٱلْأَمْوَالِ وَٱلْأَنفُسِ وَٱلثَّمَرَاتِ ۗ وَبَشِّرِ ٱلصَّابِرِينَ ۝
ٱلَّذِينَ إِذَآ أَصَابَتْهُم مُّصِيبَةٌ قَالُوٓا۟ إِنَّا لِلَّهِ وَإِنَّآ إِلَيْهِ رَاجِعُونَ ۝
أُو۟لَٰٓئِكَ عَلَيْهِمْ صَلَوَاتٌ مِّن رَّبِّهِمْ وَرَحْمَةٌ ۖ
وَأُو۟لَٰٓئِكَ هُمُ ٱلْمُهْتَدُونَ ۝

Be sure We shall test you with something of fear and hunger, some loss in goods, lives, and the produce of your work. But give good news to those who patiently carry on. Those who, when upset with tragedy, say, 'To Allah we belong, and to Him is our return.' They are those on whom descend blessings from their Lord, and mercy. They are the ones who receive guidance."

(Surah al-Baqarah 2:155-157)

القرآن

The Sahabah
Stars of Guidance

Looking Ahead

Like him, Prophet Muhammad ﷺ said the *Sahabah* were the guardians of the nation:

"The stars are a guard of the sky, if they are gone, the sky cannot escape what is ordained; and I am a safeguard to my companions, if I am not there, their fate will befall them; and they are a safeguard to my nation; if they are gone, my nation will have what is doomed for them."

(Muslim)

Rasulullah ﷺ was the final Prophet and he brought the Qur'an, the final Revelation. He came to teach mankind the best way of life and the *Sahabah* were his most devoted students. Allah ﷻ arranged that through the *Sahabah*, his mission was continued and his Message was properly understood for us today.

The *Sahabah* of Rasulullah ﷺ were a unique group of people known for their dedication and sacrifice. They are most worthy of our love and are beautiful models for us to emulate. Their acceptance of Islam and their sacrifices strengthened our faith and even after their demise, their mission continues.

Just like the stars that illuminate their surroundings, the *Sahabah* too brightened the people around them with the light of

their guidance which they received from Rasulullah ﷺ. This is the message of the *Hadith* that we have just read above.

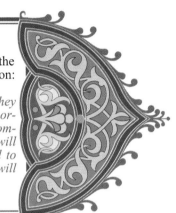

RECALL ZONE!

The *Sahabah* were the best students of Rasulullah ﷺ

- The *Sahabah* sacrificed for the sake of Islam.
- They utilized every opportunity to spread the *Din* of Allah ﷻ.

The *Sahabah* were generally those who accepted Islam in the lifetime of Rasulullah ﷺ and who met him. They struggled against the *Kuffar* to fight disbelief. They were blessed by the company of Rasulullah ﷺ. They loved each other for the sake of Allah ﷻ. They sincerely believed in Him, worshipped Him and asked favors only from Him.

Meeting Rasulullah ﷺ, accepting Islam directly from him and spending even a little time with him, distinguished the *Sahabah* from all other human beings. Rasulullah ﷺ confirmed the superiority of his *Sahabah* and appointed them as our guides and leaders.

For their commitment and sacrifice to Islam, Allah ﷻ praised them and promised them paradise in the '*Akhirah*. Do you know that the *Sahabah*'s excellent position can be found in the Qur'an?

وَٱلسَّٰبِقُونَ ٱلْأَوَّلُونَ مِنَ ٱلْمُهَٰجِرِينَ وَٱلْأَنصَارِ وَٱلَّذِينَ ٱتَّبَعُوهُم بِإِحْسَٰنٍ رَّضِىَ ٱللَّهُ عَنْهُمْ وَرَضُوا۟ عَنْهُ وَأَعَدَّ لَهُمْ جَنَّٰتٍ تَجْرِى تَحْتَهَا ٱلْأَنْهَٰرُ خَٰلِدِينَ فِيهَآ أَبَدًا ذَٰلِكَ ٱلْفَوْزُ ٱلْعَظِيمُ ۞

"And the first to lead the way of Islam, the Muhajirun and the Ansar, and those who followed them in goodness- Allah is well-pleased with them and they are well-pleased with Him, and He has made ready for them gardens under which rivers flow, where they will dwell forever. That is the supreme triumph."

(Surah al-Tawbah: 100)

The *Muhajirun* of Makkah faced hardships in their own city. They sacrificed whatever they had for freedom from the persecution of the Quraish. When they reached Madinah, the *Ansar* willingly took them in and shared their wealth and resources with them. The verse also mentioned other Muslims who did good for others only for the sake of Allah ﷻ. Their love for the *Din* and their sacrifices are a model for us today.

Islam appealed to people from all walks of life. As such, the *Sahabah* consisted of the weak and the strong, poor slaves and rich masters, Arabs and non-Arabs, men and women and young and old. Not all of the *Sahabah* accepted Islam at the same time. The number of *Sahabah* expanded gradually.

The *Sahabah* devoted their lives to the cause of truth. Their faith in Allah ﷻ and Rasulullah ﷺ made them truly inspiring models for us. *Inshallah*, just like the *Sahabah* and *Sahabiyah*, we will be the stars guiding the *Ummah*.

WE HAVE LEARNED:

- Despite the differences among the *Sahabah*, they were united in their struggle for Islam.
- This unity brought them together as they showed extreme love and affection for Rasulullah ﷺ.

WORDS TO KNOW:

Illuminate, Utilize, Commitment, Devoted

32 Lesson

Looking Ahead

Euripides a famous ancient Greek poet once wrote:

"To a father growing old, nothing is dearer than a daughter."

Let's read about the beloved daughter of Rasulullah ﷺ and her place in his life.

Sayyidatina Fatimah ؓ was the youngest daughter of Rasulullah ﷺ from his first wife, Khadijah ؓ. She had three older sisters Zaynab, Ruqqiyyah and Ummu Kulthum ؓ.

She was born in the year when the Ka'bah was damaged by a flood and her noble father was fated to resolve the conflict by the tribal leaders regarding the *Hajr Aswad*, the Black Stone.

Sayyidatina Fatimah ؓ was five years old when Angel Jibril ؑ revealed the first *Wahi* to her Blessed father. Rasulullah ﷺ gave the good news of Allah's message to his family and close relatives first. He told them that they should worship only One God from now on. Khadijah ؓ was the first one to accept and explain it to her daughters.

Fatimah ؓ became even closer to her father since then. She would often accompany him when he would go to the Ka'bah or walk through the streets of Makkah. Once when she was at Ka'bah with her father a group of men including Abu Jahl ibn Hisham, came and stood around him as he was praying. Abu Jahl asked, "who will bring the bloody guts of a slaughtered sheep and throw it on Muhammad?" One of the men went away and returned with the filth and threw it on the shoulders of Rasulullah ﷺ as he was making *Sajdah*.

Fatimah ؓ was extremely sad to see her dear father being treated in such an unacceptable manner. She rushed to him and cleaned all the filth from his shoulders. She saw such rude behavior of the Quraish against her father and other Muslims many times. It hurt her deeply but she became strong and firm in her defense of her noble father and his Faith.

Sayyidatina Fatimah grew up learning and living Islam as it was revealed, taught and practiced by the best of the teachers. Fatimah ؏ and her sisters were the first generation of Muslims raised in the blessed household of Rasulullah ﷺ and Khadijah ؏.

In our society, at seven years old, we would most probably be in school. At that age, Sayyidatina Fatimah ؏ learned the meaning of the words "to suffer from hunger" when the tribe of Bani Hashim was boycotted by the Makkans and the entire family had to live in the deserted valley of Abu Talib. Those were very difficult three years for the entire family but they remained patient and trusted Allah ﷻ.

Her mother, Sayyidatina Khadijah ؏ became very ill after the boycott of three years. Her death was difficult for the entire family, especially young Fatimah ؏ who was only 15 years old.

After the death of her mother Sayyidatina Fatimah ؏ began to spend more time with her father, taking care of him and learning from him. She was so concerned about his well-being that she was called "Umm Abiha" (the mother of her father). Prophet ﷺ loved her dearly and once said;

"Whoever pleases Fatimah has indeed pleased God and whoever has caused her to be angry has indeed angered God. Fatimah is a part of me. Whatever pleases

her pleases me and whatever angers her angers me."

(Muslim)

Sayyidatina Fatimah ؏ traveled to Madinah and was pleased to be safe there with her father and the other believers. She became a beautiful young lady, loved and admired by everyone.

Soon after Sayyidatina Fatimah's migration to Madinah, her father began to receive proposals for her marriage from the respected men in the community. Prophet ﷺ accepted one proposal and agreed to marry his youngest daughter to young Ali ؏.

Rasulullah ﷺ himself performed the blessed marriage. It was a beautiful wedding. It is narrated that Prophet ﷺ presented Fatimah ؏ and 'Ali ؏ with a wooden bed, a blanket, a leather cushion, a sheepskin, and a stone for grinding grains to make flour.

Fatimah ؏ and 'Ali ؏ lived a very simple life. She was very loving towards her family. She respected and obeyed her husband as he also respected her wisdom and intelligence. Together they had five children - Hasan ؏, Husain ؏, Umm Kulthum ؏, Zainab ؏ and Muhsin, who died as a baby.

Sometime after the marriage, Rasulullah ﷺ gave Sayyidatina Fatimah ؏ and her husband a house near his own. He would visit her often, and her home was the first place he would go after prayer or when he returned to the city from a journey or a battle.

When her father passed away, Sayyidatina Fatimah's heart was broken. One *Sahabah* even commented that he did not see her laugh even once after that. However, Rasulullah ﷺ did tell her that she would be the first one from his family to join him in the next world.

Needless to say, six months after Rasulullah ﷺ left this life, in the blessed month of Ramadan, Sayyidatina Fatimah ؓ became very sick. Soon it was impossible for her to leave her bed. One day, she turned her face to the Qiblah and closed her eyes. She had, with such serenity and bliss, passed on to the next life.

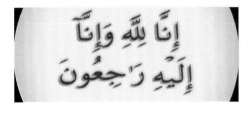

Sayyidatina Fatimah ؓ had a beaming face that seemed to radiate light, thus, giving her the title of "Az-Zahra", the "Resplendent One". She was said to have resembled Rasulullah ﷺ most in terms of appearance and personality. Sayyidatina Fatimah ؓ had very high manners and pleasant speech. She was especially kind to the poor and would often give all the food she had to those who needed it and would remain hungry herself.

Like her parents, this beautiful daughter of Rasulullah ﷺ was also a very generous woman. She never kept anything for herself, preferring instead to share with the poor and hungry.

There was once when a *Bedouin* in shabby clothes came to see Rasulullah ﷺ, asking for food and clothes. Rasulullah ﷺ sent him to Sayyidatina Fatimah's house.

Sayyidatina Fatimah ؓ received her guest but she had nothing to give him as there was nothing in her house! At first, she gave him the only sheepskin that she owned but the *Bedouin* said he could not do anything with the sheepskin.

Sayyidatina Fatimah ؓ went to search high and low for something else to give until she remembered that once her aunt gave her a gold necklace. Without thinking twice, she took off the necklace and gave it to the *Bedouin*. The *Bedouin* sold the necklace to a noble *Sahabi* named Ammar ibn Yassir ؓ, who then presented it as a gift to Rasulullah ﷺ. Rasulullah ﷺ recognized the gift and sent the necklace to Sayyidatina Fatimah ؓ who was very happy to see it again.

In spite of being busy with her young children, household chores, and taking care of the people in the community, Sayyidatina Fatimah ؓ spent her time in remembering Allah and worshipping Him. She would stay awake many nights to offer *Salah* and *Zikr*. Her devotion to Allah ﷻ and obedience to Him remained firm in spite many hardships in everyday life.

Sayyidatina Fatimah ؓ became a teacher of Muslims in the community, who would come to her with their questions and queries. Sometimes she would even visit the houses of the Muslims where women will gather to learn from her. Sayyidatina Fatimah 🕊 was a devoted teacher and educator of the members of the community, specially women and children.

The women of Madinah would come to her and learn their Din from her. They also sought her advice on various matters relating to family and children.

A SPECIAL GIFT

'Ali 🕊 and Fatimah 🕊 lived a very simple life. They did not have much money at all. Fatimah's life with 'Ali 🕊 was harder than her life in her father's house where at least she had some people to help her with her work and she did not have the responsibility of the entire household and young children.

Once her hands got blisters by grinding the grains. She said to 'Ali 🕊, "I have ground until my hands are blistered." He told her to go to her father and ask him if he can give her one of the prisoners of war as a servant to help."

She went to the Prophet 🕊. But she was very reluctant to ask him for a servant. The Prophet 🕊 asked her, "What has brought you here my dear daughter?" She answered, "I have come here to give the greetings of peace father!"

She did not have the courage to ask for what she had intended to say. Then 'Ali 🕊 and Fatimah 🕊 both decided to go together to the Prophet 🕊 and tell him what they needed.

When they told the Prophet 🕊 what they needed he told them that they were less in need of help than the other poor Muslims. He talked about Ahl al-Suffah being more in need of help than 'Ali 🕊 and Fatimah 🕊. They went back home.

Rasulullah 🕊 came to their home that night and sat down beside them. He said, "Shall I not tell you of something better than that which you asked of me?"

'Ali 🕊 and Fatimah 🕊 wanted to hear the Prophet 🕊 very much. The Prophet 🕊 said,

"These words are words that Jibril taught me: that you should say Subhan Allah (Glory to Allah), 33 times and 33 times Alhamdulillah (Praises be to Allah) and 34 times 'Allahu Akbar" (God is Great) after every prayer."
(Sahih Muslim)

'Ali 🕊 and Fatimah 🕊 were very pleased with this very special gift from Prophet 🕊. They never forgot to say the *Tasbihat* since they learned it from Rasulullah 🕊

WE HAVE LEARNED:

- Fatimah ؏ was the youngest daughter of Muhammad ﷺ and Khadijah ؏.
- Fatimah ؏ resembled her father in her speech and mannerism.
- The father and the daughter had a special bond of love and affection.
- She was married to Ali ؏, the young cousin of Rasulullah ﷺ.
- Fatimah ؏ was an intelligent and educated woman.
- She spent her life looking after her father, her family and taking care of the community in Madinah.
- She was extremely generous and kind person.
- Ali ؏ and Fatimah ؏ had five children. Hasan ؏, Husain ؏, Zainab ؏ and Umm Kulthum ؏. The youngest son, Muhsin passed away when he was was a baby.
- Prophet ﷺ called her "the leader of the young ladies of paradise."

WORDS TO KNOW:

Ancient, Turbulence, Witness, Shield, Curious

Sayyidina Bilal Ibn Rab'ah ﷺ

Looking Ahead

Have you ever wondered where the *Adhan* came from? Let's read in this lesson about the man whose name became attached to it forever.

Sayyidina Bilal ibn Rab'ah ﷺ, the first *Mu'adhdhin* of Islam, was one of the most trusted *Sahabah* of Rasulullah ﷺ. He was born in Makkah to parents who were slaves of Umayyah ibn Khalaf, a rich and powerful leader, who later became one of the biggest enemies of Islam.

Sayyidina Bilal's parents were originally from Ethiopia, a land in East Africa. When they were small, they were captured and brought back to Arabia. They were sold as slave in the market place. In those days the children of slaves were considered slaves too until someone freed them. So, Sayyidina Bilal ﷺ too was a slave of Umayyah.

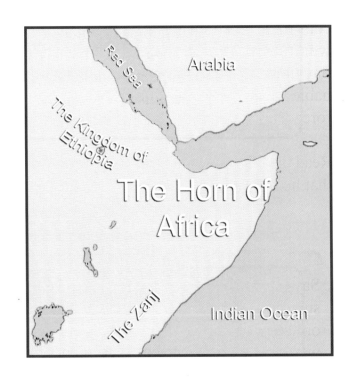

Sayyidina Bilal ﷺ grew up in very difficult situation as a slave. His master wanted to keep him strong and alive, but at the same time, he ignored his rights and dignity. He was seen as valuable property that could work and earn money for his master.

When Sayyidina Bilal ﷺ heard the teachings of Rasulullah ﷺ, he became very interested. As he heard more he became convinced of the truth of Rasulullah's mission. Bilal's heart responded to the message of the Prophet ﷺ and he recited the *Shahadah* and became one of the most devoted *Sahabah* of Rasulullah. In fact, he was the seventh person to embrace Islam. That is why he is known as one of the *as-Sabiqun al-awwalun* which means the "First Ones". These people suffered a great deal, especially at the hands of the Makkans. Sayyidina Bilal ﷺ was no exception.

Since he was a slave, Sayyidina Bilal ﷺ still had to serve his master. So strong was his belief in Islam, that he did not keep his conversion a secret. His master Umayyah was furious and began to torture Sayyidina Bilal ﷺ in the most unimaginable ways. His master hoped he could force Bilal ﷺ to return to idol-worship.

Read the following to discover the tortures that he put Bilal ﷺ through:

Sayyidina Bilal ﷺ was dressed in a suit of metal armor and then taken out on the desert in the hot sun where he was made to lie on the burning sand at mid-day. The heated metal scorched his skin. There were times when he fell unconscious from the pain.

A huge boulder was placed on Bilal's chest. While it slowly crushed him, he was asked all sorts of sarcastic questions like "Do you believe in the goddess al-Lat?" or "Do you believe in the goddess 'Uzza?" or "Why doesn't your God come and save you now?"

However, despite all the tortures and taunts, Sayyidina Bilal ﷺ did not give in to his master's demands to continue worshiping the stone idols.

Yet, Sayyidina Bilal ﷺ was a strong man, physically and spiritually. He had a strong body and a stronger heart which protected his faith. Through the agonizing pain and suffering, his lips kept uttering over and over, "Allah is One...Allah is One... *Ahad...Ahad...Ahad...*"

One day, while Umayyah was torturing Sayyidina Bilal ﷺ, Sayyidina Abu Bakr ﷺ came upon the scene. He was shocked at what he witnessed. He immediately asked Umayyah if he could buy Sayyidina Bilal's freedom. Umayyah asked for a very high price which Abu Bakr ﷺ agreed upon.

The two men went to meet Rasulullah ﷺ to inform him of the good news. Sayyidina Abu Bakr ﷺ announced, "I am setting Bilal free, O Messenger of Allah!" Rasulullah ﷺ was very happy and with that, Sayyidina Bilal ﷺ became a free man.

Sayyidina Bilal ﷺ loved the Prophet ﷺ deeply. He migrated to Madinah along with the other *Sahabah*. He became one of the *Ashab us-Suffah,* People of the Bench, who stayed in Al- Masjid un-Nabawi and learnt from Rasulullah ﷺ. He was a witness to Rasulullah's perfect character.

Sayyidina Bilal ﷺ was a humble man who did not seek fame for his deeds. Allah ﷻ gave him a virtuous nature and he remained modest and humble all his life. He was the kind of man who would not speak unless he was spoken to. His heart was full of love and affection for Rasulullah ﷺ and he was Rasulullah's devoted *sahabi*.

Rasulullah ﷺ once said to Sayyidina Bilal ﷺ, "Tell me, what act have you done for which you hope to receive a special reward from Allah? Because last night I dreamt I heard your footsteps in front of me in the Jannah." Sayyidina Bilal ﷺ responded, "I haven't done anything special recently except for this: Whenever I make my Wudu' during the night or day I pray two Rakat's in honor of that purification."

Rasulullah ﷺ entrusted Sayyidina Bilal ﷺ with the management of the finances of the Muslim community in Madinah. He was also appointed by Rasullullah ﷺ to be the first Mu'adhdhan ever. He was given the honor of being the first person in the history of Islam to call Muslims to perform *Salat*.

Sayyidina Bilal ﷺ loved the Prophet ﷺ so much that after his death he could not

- Bilal ﷺ was a slave who belonged to Umayyah ibn Khallaf. He was severely tortured by Umayyah after embracing Islam.

- Abu Bakr ﷺ bought him from Umayyah and set him free which made Rasulullah ﷺ very happy.

bring himself to make the *Adhan* anymore. He even left Madinah out of sadness and went to live in a village that was far away. However, one night, Sayyidina Bilal ﷺ had a dream in which Rasulullah ﷺ appeared to him and said, "O Bilal! Why do you never visit me?"

The next day, after the Fajr prayer, he set out for Madinah. When he got there, he met Hazrat Hasan ﷺ and Hazrat Husain ﷺ, the grandsons of Rasulullah ﷺ. When they saw Sayyidina Bilal ﷺ they pleaded with him to make the *Adhan* like he used to when Rasulullah ﷺ was still alive. He loved these two so much that he could not refuse their request.

STORY OF THE FIRST *ADHAN*

In Makkah the number of Muslims was small. When Rasulullah ﷺ arrived in Madinah, the number of Muslims started to increase. By the second year of the *Hijrah,* the number of Muslims had increased. The people announced in a loud voice, *"As-salat ul-Jami'ah,* the *Salah* for *Jama'ah* is ready."* Those who heard this call came to join the *Salah.* Muslims felt the need for a better way to inform people to come to *Salah.* Rasulullah ﷺ asked his *Sahabah* for their advice.

Some *Sahabah* suggested that Muslims, like the Jews, should blow a horn to announce the time for the *Salah.* Others said the Muslims might ring bells like the Christians do in their Churches. A few proposed that the Muslims kindle a fire to call people to pray. Rasulullah ﷺ was not satisfied with any of these ideas. He waited to hear a better idea or to receive guidance from Allah ﷻ.

One day, a *Sahabi* named Abdullah ibn Zaid ﵁, came to Rasulullah ﷺ and said, "O Messenger of Allah! I had a beautiful dream last night".

"What was the dream you saw?" Rasulullah ﷺ asked Ibn Zaid ﵁.

He answered, "I saw a man wearing white garments teaching me the words to call people to prayer with". He then recited the words for the *Adhan.*

The words were beautiful and full of meaning. Rasulullah ﷺ recognized that the dream of Abdullah ibn Zaid ﵁ was true. He asked Abdullah ﵁ to teach the words of *Adhan* to Bilal ﵁, who had a loud and beautiful voice.

Bilal ﵁ stood up and called the *Adhan.* His voice resounded throughout Madinah. People came running to Masjid un-Nabi. Rasulullah ﷺ accepted this *Adhan* as the official call to the *Salah.* Bilal ﵁ became the first *Mu'adhdhin* of Islam.

Sayyidina Bilal ؓ climbed once again to the rooftop of the Masjid an-Nabawi and called out the *Adhan*. When the people heard his voice after many long years, both men and women came running out of their houses weeping. They remembered the days when Rasulullah ﷺ walked the earth. But this was the last *Adhan* ever heard in Madinah from the first *Mu'adhdhin*.

After he made this last *Adhan*, Sayyidina Bilal ؓ left the Arabian Peninsula. He eventually made his way to the great city of Damascus, which was far away in Syria. He lived with a number of other *Sahabi* who had moved there. Yet in his heart was a deep pain. He yearned to be with the beloved Rasulullah ﷺ again. On his death bed, he said, "Tomorrow, you will meet your loved ones, Muhammad and his companions." He died in Damascus in 20H. His blessed grave still stands in the old section of the city and many Believers come to visit him.

THE PRAYER AFTER THE ADHAN
Narrated by Jabir bin 'Abdullah, Allah's ﷺ Apostle said,
"Whoever, after listening to the Azan says,

اَللّٰهُمَّ رَبَّ هٰذِهِ الدَّعْوَةِ التَّآمَّةِ وَ الصَّلاةِ الْقَآئِمَةِ اٰتِ
سَيِّدَنَا مُحَمَّدَ نِالْوَسِيلَةَ وَ الْفَضِيلَةَ وَ الدَّرَجَةَ الرَّفِيعَةَ
وَ الْبَعْثُهُ مَقَامًا مَّحْمُودَا الَّذِى وَعَدْتَّهُ وَارْزُقْنَا شَفَاعَتَهُ
يَوْمَ الْقِيَامَةِ إِنَّكَ لَا تُخْلِفُ الْمِيْعَادِ

O Allah! Lord of this perfect call (of not ascribing partners to You) and of the regular prayer which is going to be established! Kindly give Muhammad the right of intercession and superiority and send him (on the Day of Judgment) to the best and the highest place in Paradise which You promised him). Then intercession for me will be permitted through him on the Day of Resurrection."
(al-Bukhari)

WE HAVE LEARNED:

- Bilal ibn Rab'ah ؓ was born in Makkah.
- His parents were from Ethiopia.
- Bilal ؓ and his parents were slaves of Umayyah ibn Khallaf.
- Abu Bakr ؓ bought Bilal's freedom from Umayyah and set him free.
- Bilal ؓ was a devoted and loving *Sahabi* of Rasulullah ﷺ.
- Rasulullah ﷺ honored him by making him the first *Mu'adhdhin* of Islam.

WORDS TO KNOW:

As-Sabiqun, Al-Awwalun, Damascus, Intercession